THIS IS OUR FAITH

Heritage Program, Book II

Author: Kate Sweeney Ristow

SILVER BURDETT & GINN
MORRISTOWN, N.J.

THIS IS OUR FAITH

Heritage Program, Book II

Consultants: Sister Mary Boys S.N.J.M., Rev. Frank Sokol, Barbara Zanin

Readers: Deborah Hawks, Judith Conte

Nihil Obstat
Reverend Anselm Murray, O.S.B.
Censor Librorum

Imprimatur
✠Most Reverend Frank J. Rodimer
Bishop of Paterson
February 17, 1989

The *nihil obstat* and *imprimatur* are official declarations that a book or pamphlet is free of doctrinal and moral error. No implication is contained therein that those who have granted the *nihil obstat* and *imprimatur* agree with contents, opinions, or statements expressed.

Acknowledgements
Excerpts from *The New American Bible with Revised New Testament* copyright © 1986 by the Confraternity of Christian Doctrine, Washington, D.C.

Excerpts from the English translation of *The Roman Missal* © 1985, International Committee on English in the Liturgy, Inc. ICLE. All rights reserved.

Excerpts from the English translation of the *Rite of Baptism of Children* © 1969 ICEL; the English translation of the *Rite of Confirmation* © 1971; the English translation of the *Rite of Reconciliation of Individual Pentitents* © 1973. All rights reserved.

CREDITS

Cover: Paul Behrens
The Life of Jesus: Paul Behrens
Other: Michael Adams, Paul Behrens, Marie DeJohn, Richard Loehle, A. Hardy Roberts, Arvis Stewart, Chris Vallo
Map: Susan Johnson

Introduction　11: Silver Burdett & Ginn.

Chapter 1　12: *l.* Treehaus Communications, Inc./Pottebaum; *r.* David Phillips for Silver Burdett & Ginn. 14: Treehaus Communications, Inc./Pottebaum. 16: Silver Burdett & Ginn. 17: Treehaus Communications, Inc./Pottebaum. 18: Silver Burdett & Ginn.

Chapter 2　22: Silver Burdett & Ginn. 23: Silver Burdett & Ginn.

Chapter 3　33: MacDonald for Silver Burdett & Ginn.

Chapter 4　36: *l.,t.r.* Silver Burdett & Ginn; *b.r.* M. MeDici for Silver Burdett & Ginn. 39: Silver Burdett & Ginn. 40: Silver Burdett & Ginn. 42: Silver Burdett & Ginn.

Chapter 5　47: Treehaus Communications, Inc./Pottebaum. 48: Bro. Andrew Marsolek, MM/Maryknoll.

Chapter 6　52: *l.* Treehaus Communications, Inc./Pottebaum; *r.* Silver Burdett & Ginn. 53: Silver Burdett & Ginn. 54: J. Gerard Smith for Silver Burdett & Ginn. 55: J. Gerard Smith for Silver Burdett & Ginn. 57: Ken Kerbs for Silver Burdett & Ginn.

Chapter 7　62: Silver Burdett & Ginn. 63: J. Gerard Smith for Silver Burdett & Ginn. 65: Treehaus Communications, Inc./Pottebaum. 66: Treehaus Communications, Inc./Pottebaum.

Chapter 8　68: Silver Burdett & Ginn. 69: Silver Burdett & Ginn. 70: *t.* Silver Burdett & Ginn; *b.* J. Gerard Smith for Silver Burdett & Ginn. 71: J. Gerard Smith for Silver Burdett & Ginn. 72: Treehaus Communications, Inc./Pottebaum. 73: Treehaus Communications, Inc./Pottebaum. 74: Treehaus Communications, Inc./Pottebaum.

Chapter 9　76: H. Armstrong Roberts. 79: Silver Burdett & Ginn. 82: Treehaus Communications, Inc./Pottebaum.

Chapter 10　85: Treehaus Communications, Inc./Pottebaum. 88: Silver Burdett & Ginn.

Amen　92: *r.* Treehaus Communications, Inc./Pottebaum. 94: Silver Burdett & Ginn. 95: J. Gerard Smith for Silver Burdett & Ginn. 96: *r.* Tonna for Silver Burdett & Ginn. 97: Tonna for Silver Burdett & Ginn. 98: J. Gerard Smith for Silver Burdett & Ginn. 99: Silver Burdett & Ginn. 100: Treehaus Communications, Inc./Pottebaum. 101: Silver Burdett & Ginn. 102: Silver Burdett & Ginn. 103: Michal Heron for Silver Burdett & Ginn. 105: Treehaus Communications, Inc./Pottebaum. 108: Silver Burdett & Ginn.

Contents

See lesson plans on pages 4T–13T of Teacher Edition. Circled numbers indicate factual questions; squared numbers are thought or reflective questions.

Explain that the Scriptures are written in chapter and verse. Help the youngsters identify these in the scriptural passages below.

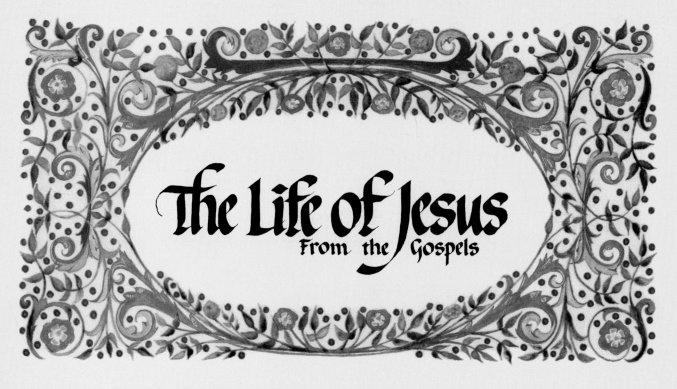

The Life of Jesus
From the Gospels

...he interpreted to them what referred to him in all the scriptures. Luke 24:27

You are going to read some stories from the gospels. They tell the story of Jesus, God's Son, our friend, our brother, our savior, and our teacher. You will discover why God sent Jesus to us. You will learn how Jesus wants us to live in the world that God made for us. It is an exciting story that never ends. It continues on in all of us who come to know and love Jesus.

The story as presented in this book does not begin at the beginning of Jesus' life. Instead, it begins after he died. In the story, two followers of Jesus are deep in conversation about him. Their minds flash back to all that he said and did. With them, you will discover important things that we believe about Jesus.

THE APPEARANCE ON THE ROAD TO EMMAUS
*Luke 24:13ff**

ow that very day two of them were going to a village seven miles from Jerusalem called Emmaus (Eh MAY uhs), ¹⁴and they were conversing about all the things that had occurred. ¹⁵And it happened that while they were

---

*The Scriptures are arranged in chapters and verses. The name of the book of Scripture appears first, followed by the chapter and verse numbers. We have included the verse numbers in the text to acquaint you with their use.

1. Why did his followers (disciples) not recognize Jesus?
2. How did the disciples say Jesus died?
3. What were the disciples hoping?
4. What had the women who visited the tomb told them?

5. How did Jesus help the disciples understand what had happened?
6. What did Jesus do with the bread?
7. What happened once the disciples recognized Jesus?

conversing and debating, Jesus himself drew near and walked

(1.) with them, ¹⁶but their eyes were prevented from recognizing him. ¹⁷He asked them, "What are you discussing as you walk along?" They stopped, looking downcast. ¹⁸One of them, named Cleopas (KLEE oh pas), said to him in reply, "Are you the only visitor to Jerusalem who does not know of the things that have taken place there in these days?" ¹⁹And he replied to them, "What sort of things?"

They said to him, "The things that happened to Jesus the Nazarene, who was a **prophet*** mighty in deed and word before God and all the people, ²⁰how our chief priests and rulers

(2.) both handed him over to a sentence of death and crucified him.

(3.) ²¹But we were hoping that he would be the one to redeem Israel; and besides all this, it is now the third day since this took place. ²²Some women from our group, however, have astounded us: they were at the tomb early in the morning ²³and did not

(4.) find his body; they came back and reported that they had indeed seen a vision of **angels*** who announced that he was alive. ²⁴Then some of those with us went to the tomb and found things just as the women had described, but him they did not see."

²⁵And he said to them, "Oh, how foolish you are! How slow of heart to believe all that the prophets spoke! ²⁶Was it not necessary that the Messiah should suffer these things and enter

(5.) into his glory?" ²⁷Then beginning with Moses and all the prophets, he interpreted to them what referred to him in all the scriptures.

²⁸As they approached the village to which they were going, he gave the impression that he was going on farther. ²⁹But they urged him, "Stay with us, for it is nearly evening and the day is almost over." So he went in to stay with them. ³⁰And it

(6.) happened that, while he was with them at table, he took bread, said the blessing, broke it, and gave it to them. ³¹With that their

(7.) eyes were opened and they recognized him, but he vanished

. . .he took bread, said the blessing, broke it, and gave it to them. Luke 24:30

prophet: someone called by God to speak in God's name
angels: messengers from God

1

1. What did the disciples do next?
2. How do you think the disciples felt when they found out that Jesus rose from the dead? (Answers will vary but may include happy and joyful.)

3. What did John the Baptist preach?
4. Why were people going to John?
5. What did John say about the one coming after him?

"This is my beloved Son, with whom I am well pleased." Matthew 3:17

from their sight. [32]Then they said to each other, "Were not our hearts burning [within us] while he spoke to us on the way and opened the scriptures to us?" [33]So they set out at once and returned to Jerusalem where they found gathered together **the eleven*** and those with them [34]who were saying, "The **Lord*** has truly been raised and has appeared to Simon!" [35]Then the two recounted what had taken place on the way and how he was made known to them in the breaking of the bread.

Jesus' followers had seen him do many wonderful things. However, they never expected anything as amazing as his rising from the dead. Can you imagine what they thought after that happened? Whenever they gathered together, they asked one another what it might mean and they read the Hebrew Scriptures to help them understand. Finally, they came to firmly believe that Jesus was truly the Son of God. Then everything that he had said and done became clearer to them.

As new members joined their group, the followers of Jesus told the stories and explained their meaning. After a while, some of the disciples wrote down all that the community believed about Jesus. We call these writings the gospel, or the good news.

You are going to read some of these stories. They tell what the followers of Jesus believed about him and what we believe today.

THE PREACHING OF JOHN THE BAPTIST
Matthew 3:1ff

n those days John the Baptist appeared, preaching in the desert of Judea [2][and] saying, "Repent, for the kingdom of heaven is at hand!"

. . . [5]At that time Jerusalem, all Judea, and the whole region around the Jordan (JORD n) were going out to him [6]and were

---

the eleven: Jesus' special followers, originally twelve; one (Judas) had died

Lord: a special name people use for God

2

6. Who was John speaking of? (Jesus)
7. Why did John try to prevent Jesus' baptism?
8. What happened after Jesus was baptized?
9. Who is Jesus? (God's Son.)

10. Who gave Jesus the power to preach?
11. Where did Jesus teach?
12. What did God send Jesus to do? (See quotation from the prophet Isaiah.)

being baptized by him in the Jordan River as they acknowledged their sins.

*John the Baptist was inspired to tell the people: ⱱ... *¹¹"I am
(5.) baptizing you with water, for **repentance,** but the one who is coming after me is mightier than I. I am not worthy to carry his sandals. He will baptize you with the holy Spirit and fire."

6.

... ¹³Then Jesus came from Galilee (GAL eh lee) to John at the
(7.) Jordan to be baptized by him. ¹⁴John tried to prevent him, saying, "I need to be baptized by you, and yet you are coming to me?" ¹⁵Jesus said to him in reply, "Allow it now, for thus it is fitting for us to fulfill all righteousness." Then he allowed him. ¹⁶After Jesus was baptized, he came up from the water and
(8.) behold, the heavens were opened [for him], and he saw the Spirit of God descending like a dove [and] coming upon him. ¹⁷And a voice came from the heavens, saying, "This is my beloved Son, with whom I am well pleased."

9.

THE BEGINNING OF THE GALILEAN MINISTRY
Luke 4:14ff

"The Spirit of the Lord is upon me,
because he has anointed me
to bring glad tidings to the poor."
Luke 4:18

(10.)
(11.) Jesus returned to Galilee in the power of the Spirit, and news of him spread throughout the whole region. ¹⁵He taught in their **synagogues** (SIHN uh gahgs) and was praised by all. ¹⁶He came to Nazareth, where he had grown up, and went according to his custom into the synagogue on the sabbath (SAB uhth) day. He stood up to read ¹⁷and was handed a scroll of the prophet Isaiah (I zai uh). He unrolled the scroll and found the passage where it was written:

(12.) ¹⁸The Spirit of the Lord is upon me,
because he has anointed me
to bring glad tidings to the poor.
He has sent me to proclaim liberty to captives
and recovery of sight to the blind,
to let the oppressed go free,
¹⁹and to proclaim a year acceptable to the Lord.

²⁰Rolling up the scroll, he handed it back to the attendant and sat down, and the eyes of all in the synagogue looked intently at him. ²¹He said to them, "Today this scripture passage is fulfilled in your hearing."

ⱱ **words not directly quoted from the Bible**
repentance: regret or sorrow for having done wrong

synagogues: local Jewish meeting places for worship and study

1. What did the lepers want Jesus to do? (Heal them.)
2. Why did one leper return to Jesus?
3. Why did Jesus say the leper had been saved?
4. How can we be like the thankful leper? (Possible answers might include having faith in Jesus and being thankful to Jesus.)
5. What did the sinful woman do for Jesus?
6. What did Simon think Jesus should know?

THE CLEANSING OF TEN LEPERS
Luke 17:11ff

 s he continued his journey to Jerusalem, he traveled through Samaria (suh mar ee ah) and Galilee. ¹²As he was entering a village, ten lepers met [him]. They stood at a distance from him ¹³and raised their voice, saying, "Jesus, Master! Have pity on us!" ¹⁴And when he saw them, he said, "Go show yourselves to the priests." As they were going they were cleansed. ¹⁵And one of them, realizing he had been healed, returned, glorifying God in a loud voice; ¹⁶and he fell at the feet of Jesus and thanked him. He was a **Samaritan.*** ¹⁷Jesus said in reply, "Ten were cleansed, were they not? Where are the other nine? ¹⁸Has none but this foreigner returned to give thanks to God?" ¹⁹Then he said to him, "Stand up and go; your faith has saved you."

4.

THE PARDON OF THE SINFUL WOMAN
Luke 7:36ff

 Pharisee* (far uh see) invited him to dine with him, and he entered the Pharisee's house and reclined at table. ³⁷Now there was a sinful woman in the city who learned that he was at table in the house of the Pharisee. Bringing an alabaster flask of ointment, ³⁸she stood behind him at his feet weeping and began to bathe his feet with her tears. Then she wiped them with her hair, kissed them, and anointed them with the ointment.

³⁹When the Pharisee who had invited him saw this he said to himself, "If this man were a prophet, he would know who and what sort of woman this is who is touching him, that she is a sinner." ⁴⁰Jesus said to him in reply, "Simon, I have something to say to you." "Tell me, teacher," he said. ⁴¹"Two people were in debt to a certain creditor; one owed five hundred days' wages and the other owed fifty. ⁴²Since they were unable to repay the debt, he forgave it for both. Which of them will love

He said to her, "Your sins are forgiven."
Luke 7:48

4

Samaritan: someone from Samaria, the land north of Jerusalem

Pharisee: deeply devout Jewish person who centered his life on Bible study and the perfect observance of God's law

7. Why did Jesus say the woman's sins were forgiven?
8. What can we learn from this story? (Answers will vary but may include that Jesus forgives sins and Jesus loves sinners.)

9. How did Jesus feel when he saw the crowd?
10. Why did the disciples want to send the crowd away?

him more?" ⁴³Simon said in reply, "The one, I suppose, whose larger debt was forgiven." He said to him, "You have judged rightly."

⁴⁴Then he turned to the woman and said to Simon (SI muhn), "Do you see this woman? When I entered your house, you did not give me water for my feet, but she has bathed them with her tears and wiped them with her hair. ⁴⁵You did not give me a kiss, but she has not ceased kissing my feet since the time I entered. ⁴⁶You did not anoint my head with oil, but she anointed my feet with ointment. ⁴⁷So I tell you, her many sins have been forgiven; hence, she has shown great love. But the one to whom little is forgiven, loves little." ⁴⁸He said to her, "Your sins are forgiven." ⁴⁹The others at table said to themselves, "Who is this who even forgives sins?" ⁵⁰But he said to the woman, "Your faith has saved you; go in peace."

THE RETURN OF THE TWELVE
Mark 6:30ff

The apostles gathered together with Jesus and reported all they had done and taught. ³¹He said to them, "Come away by yourselves to a deserted place and rest a while." People were coming and going in great numbers, and they had no opportunity even to eat. ³²So they went off in the boat by themselves to a deserted place. ³³People saw them leaving and many came to know about it. They hastened there on foot from all the towns and arrived at the place before them.

THE FEEDING OF THE FIVE THOUSAND
Mark 6:34ff

When he disembarked and saw the vast crowd, his heart was moved with pity for them, for they were like sheep without a shepherd; and he began to teach them many things. ³⁵By now it was already late and his disciples approached him and said, "This is a deserted place and it is already very late.

He . . . broke the loaves and gave them to [his] disciples to set before the people . . . . Mark 6:41

5

1. What did Jesus do with the food?
2. How can we imitate Jesus? (We can care about others.)
3. Who wanted to put Jesus to death?
4. Which one of the disciples betrayed Jesus?
5. How much was Judas paid for betraying Jesus?

 36Dismiss them so that they can go to the surrounding farms and villages and buy themselves something to eat." 37He said to them in reply, "Give them some food yourselves." But they said to him, "Are we to buy two hundred days' wages worth of food and give it to them to eat?" 38He asked them, "How many loaves do you have? Go and see." And when they had found out they said, "Five loaves and two fish." 39So he gave orders to have them sit down in groups on the green grass. 40The people took their places in rows by hundreds and by fifties.

(1.) 41Then, taking the five loaves and the two fish and looking up to heaven, he said the blessing, broke the loaves, and gave them to [his] disciples to set before the people; he also divided the two fish among them all. 42They all ate and were satisfied. 43And they picked up twelve wicker baskets full of fragments and what was left of the fish. 44Those who ate [of the loaves] were five thousand men.

THE PASSION (Part I)

THE CONSPIRACY AGAINST JESUS
Matthew 26:1ff

When Jesus finished all these words, he said to his disciples, 2"You know that in two days' time it will be **Passover,*** and the Son of Man will be handed over (3.) to be crucified." 3Then the chief priests and the elders of the people assembled in the palace of the high priest, who was called Caiaphas (KAI uh fuhs), 4and they consulted together to arrest Jesus by treachery and put him to death.

They paid him thirty pieces of silver, and from that time on he looked for an opportunity to hand him over.
Matthew 26:15–16

THE BETRAYAL OF JESUS
Matthew 26:14ff

(4.) **T**hen one of the Twelve, who was called Judas Iscariot (Ih SCAR ee uht), went to the chief priests 15and said, "What are you willing to give me if I hand him over (5.) to you?" They paid him thirty pieces of silver, 16and from that time on he looked for an opportunity to hand him over.

Passover: the Jewish feast celebrating God's freeing the Jews from slavery in Egypt

6. What did Jesus say when he broke the bread?
7. What did Jesus say when he took the cup?

8. How did Jesus feel as his death approached?
9. What did Jesus tell his father?
10. Why did Jesus pray at this time? (He knew that he was going to suffer and die.)

THE LAST SUPPER
Luke 22:14ff

 When the hour came, he took his place at table with the apostles. ¹⁵He said to them, "I have eagerly desired to eat this Passover with you before I suffer, ¹⁶for, I tell you, I shall not eat it [again] until there is fulfillment in the kingdom of God." ¹⁷Then he took a cup, gave thanks, and said, "Take this and share it among yourselves; ¹⁸for I tell you [that] from this time on I shall not drink of the fruit of the vine until the kingdom of God comes." ¹⁹Then he took the bread, said the blessing, broke it, and gave it to them, saying, "This is my body, which will be given for you; do this in memory of me." ²⁰And likewise the cup after they had eaten, saying, "This cup is the new **covenant*** in my blood, which will be shed for you."

THE PASSION (Part II)

THE AGONY IN THE GARDEN
Matthew 26:36ff

 Then Jesus came with them to a place called Gethsemane, and he said to his disciples, "Sit here while I go over there and pray." ³⁷He took along Peter and the two sons of Zebedee, and began to feel sorrow and distress. ³⁸Then he said to them, "My soul is sorrowful even to death. Remain here and keep watch with me." ³⁹He advanced a little and fell prostrate in prayer, saying, "My Father, if it is possible, let this cup pass from me; yet, not as I will, but as you will." ⁴⁰When he returned to his disciples he found them asleep. He said to Peter, "So you could not keep watch with me for one hour? ⁴¹Watch and pray that you may not undergo the test. The spirit is willing, but the flesh is weak." ⁴²Withdrawing a second time, he prayed again, "My Father, if it is not possible that this cup pass without my drinking it, your will be done!" ⁴³Then he returned once more and found them asleep, for they could not keep their eyes open. ⁴⁴He left them and withdrew again and prayed a third time, saying the same thing again. ⁴⁵Then he returned to his disciples and said to them, "Are you still sleeping and taking your rest? Behold, the hour is at hand when the Son of Man is to be handed over to sinners. ⁴⁶Get up, let us go. Look, my betrayer is at hand."

"Take and eat; this is my body."
Matthew 26:26

10.

covenant: an agreement or contract between two people or groups

7

1. How did Judas betray Jesus?
2. Who did the high priest say Jesus was claiming to be?
3. What did the people say when Jesus said he would soon be with God the Father? (*The Power* means God.)

THE BETRAYAL AND ARREST OF JESUS
Matthew 26:47ff

While he was still speaking, Judas, one of the Twelve, arrived, accompanied by a large crowd, with swords and clubs, who had come from the chief priests and the elders of the people. ⁴⁸His betrayer had arranged a sign with them saying, "The man I shall kiss is the one; arrest him."

. . . ⁵⁷Those who had arrested Jesus led him away to Caiaphas the high priest, where the scribes and the elders were assembled.

. . . ⁵⁹The chief priests and the entire **Sanhedrin*** (San HED rehn) kept trying to obtain false testimony against Jesus in order to put him to death, ⁶⁰but they found none, though many false witnesses came forward.

. . . ⁶³But Jesus was silent. Then the high priest said to him, "I order you to tell us under oath before the living God whether you are the **Messiah*** (Meh SI ah), the Son of God." ⁶⁴Jesus said to him in reply,
"You have said so. But I tell you:
From now on you will see 'the Son of Man seated at the right hand of the Power'
and 'coming on the clouds of heaven.' "
⁶⁵Then the high priest tore his robes and said, "He has blasphemed! What further need have we of witnesses? You have now heard the **blasphemy***; ⁶⁶what is your opinion?" They said in reply, "He deserves to die!"

JESUS BEFORE PILATE
Matthew 27:1ff

When it was morning, all the chief priests and the elders of the people took counsel against Jesus to put him to death. ²They bound him, led him away, and handed him over to Pilate (PIE luht), the governor.

. . . ¹¹Now Jesus stood before the governor, and he questioned him, "Are you the king of the Jews?" Jesus said, "You say so." ¹²And when he was accused by the chief priests and elders, he made no answer. ¹³Then Pilate said to him, "Do you not hear how many things they are testifying against you?" ¹⁴But he did not answer him one word, so that the governor was amazed.

. . . "I am innocent of this man's blood. Look to it yourselves." Matthew 27:24

Sanhedrin: the religious, civil, and criminal court of the Jews during the time of Jesus
Messiah: the one God had promised to send to bring peace, love, and justice
blasphemy: an insult to God or claim to do what only God does

4. Why did Pilate not want to be responsible for Jesus' death? (He did not think that Jesus had done anything wrong.)
5. What did Pilate do?

6. What did the centurion and other soldiers say about Jesus?

¹⁵Now on the occasion of the feast the governor was accustomed to release to the crowd one prisoner whom they wished.

Pilate was hoping they would call for the release of Jesus.† ²²Pilate said to them, "Then what shall I do with Jesus called Messiah?" They all said, "Let him be crucified!" ²³But he said, "Why? What evil has he done?" They only shouted the louder, "Let him be crucified!" ²⁴When Pilate saw that he was not succeeding at all, but that a riot was breaking out instead, he took water and washed his hands in the sight of the crowd, saying, "I am innocent of this man's blood. Look to it yourselves.". . . ²⁶Then he released Barabbas (bah RAB bihs) to them, but after he had Jesus scourged, he handed him over to be crucified.

THE CRUCIFIXION
Matthew 27:33ff

And when they came to a place called Golgotha (GAUL gih thuh) (which means Place of the Skull), ³⁴they gave Jesus wine to drink mixed with gall. But when he had tasted it, he refused to drink. ³⁵After they had crucified him, they divided his garments by casting lots. . . .

³⁹Those passing by reviled him, shaking their heads and saying, "You who would destroy the temple and rebuild it in three days, save yourself, if you are the Son of God, [and] come down from the cross!"

. . . ⁴⁵From noon onward, darkness came over the whole land until three in the afternoon. ⁴⁶And about three o'clock Jesus cried out in a loud voice, *"Eli, Eli, lema sabachthani?"* which means, "My God, my God, why have you forsaken me?"

. . . ⁵⁴The **centurion*** and the men with him who were keeping watch over Jesus feared greatly when they saw the earthquake and all that was happening, and they said, "Truly, this was the Son of God!"

"Father, forgive them, they know not what they do." Luke 23:34

† words not directly quoted from the Bible
centurion: an officer in the Roman army

1. What did the men in dazzling garments tell them?
2. What did the women do?
3. How does the good news of Jesus' resurrection make you feel? (Possible answers might include being joyous, hopeful, glad to belong to his Church.)
4. What work did Jesus give the disciples to do?

THE RESURRECTION OF JESUS
Luke 24:1ff

ut at daybreak on the first day of the week they took the spices they had prepared and went to the tomb. ²They found the stone rolled away from the tomb; ³but when they entered, they did not find the body of the Lord Jesus. ⁴While they were puzzling over this, behold, two men in dazzling garments appeared to them. ⁵They were terrified and bowed their faces to the ground. They said to them, "Why do you seek the living one among the dead? ⁶He is not here, but he has been raised. Remember what he said to you while he was still in Galilee, ⁷that the Son of Man must be handed over to sinners and be crucified, and rise on the third day." ⁸And they remembered his words.

②⁹Then they returned from the tomb and announced all these things to the eleven and to all the others.

③

THE COMMISSIONING OF THE DISCIPLES
Matthew 28:16ff

he eleven disciples went to Galilee, to the mountain to which Jesus had ordered them. ¹⁷When they saw him, they worshiped, but they doubted. ¹⁸Then Jesus approached and said to them, "All power in heaven and on earth has been given to me. ¹⁹Go, therefore, and make disciples of all nations, baptizing them in the name of the Father, and of the Son, and of the holy Spirit, ²⁰teaching them to observe all that I have commanded you. And behold, I am with you always, until the end of the age."

. . . They did not find the body of the Lord Jesus. Luke 24:3

Introduction

WE HEAR THE GOOD NEWS

We are the people who hear the good news of Jesus! We are the people who hear and believe! Jesus' story is our story. It shows us how Jesus went about doing the work of God, his Father. The good news is that Jesus loves us and brings his love, peace, and justice to all he meets this very day.

The good news is meant to be shared, and we want to share it with you in this book. *This Is Our Faith Heritage II* will help you learn more about Jesus and the reasons he came to be with us. It will help you to understand more about the Catholic Church. It tells us how our Church — the Catholic Church — began and how it has grown. You will see what Catholics believe and how Catholics act. You will find many different ways to pray, alone or with others. With the help of other members of our Church, your belief in God, Jesus, the Holy Spirit, and the Church will begin to grow.

Jesus once told a story about the mustard seed, the smallest seed of all. He pointed out that from this tiny seed a large bush grows, tall and strong enough for birds to build nests in the branches. Your faith can grow just like the mustard seed grows. As your faith grows, you can share the good news with others and tell them about God's love for each of us.

That is what this book is all about — learning about our faith and learning how to live and share our faith. As you learn how to become a disciple of Jesus in the Church today, we hope you will discover that faith can help you to recognize your own goodness and specialness. There is no one like you and nothing like the life that Jesus invites us to!

1

See lesson plans on pages 16T–17T of Teacher Edition.
Circled numbers indicate factual questions; squared numbers are thought or reflective questions.

We Believe in God

GETTING TO KNOW YOU

Imagine that you are being interviewed for a profile in *Famous People* magazine. The reporter tells you that she wants her readers to get to know the real you. A copy of her outline for the interview she will conduct with you is found below. Write your responses in the spaces provided.

Answers will vary according to youngster's preferences.

ACTIVITY

Name _____

Birthdate _____ Birthplace _____

A humorous event I remember _____

_____

My most secret desire _____

_____

What I like best about myself _____

_____

The person I would like to be like

_____

I wonder about _____

_____

Two important people in my life

_____

_____

Name three things that you think are important in forming a relationship with another person.

Answers will vary. Possible responses might include

honesty, openness, trust, loyalty, or spending time

together.

1. What is the Bible?
2. What does the Old Testament tell us?
3. What does the New Testament tell us?

4. What is the purpose of the Scripture stories?
5. How did God establish a special relationship with us?
6. How are we like God?

✠ GOD'S RELATIONSHIP WITH ALL PEOPLE

The relationship between God and people began at Creation, when God created the universe, our world, the seas, and all living beings. We learn of God's act of creation in the **Bible**, or Scriptures.

1. The Bible is the book of God's word to us. In the Bible we learn about God, about ourselves, and about the world. Through the Bible we are able to trace the history of God's relationship with us.

The Bible is divided into two major sections:

2. the Old and the New Testaments. The Old Testament, or Hebrew Scriptures, tells us of God's relationship with the Jewish people. God chose the Jewish people to spread the truth about God throughout the world. We believe that the Jewish people are our ancestors in faith and that their

3. story is our story. The New Testament tells us about how Jesus and the first communities of his followers continued God's plan for the world.

As you read the Bible, you will discover many different forms of writing: history, biography, prophecy, and correspondence are only a few of the literary styles or forms you will find. Some of the Bible's authors wrote great symbolic sagas, while others were inspired to express God's word poetically. None of these literary forms is meant

4. to be scientifically accurate. Their purpose is to teach us about God's great love and about our relationship with God.

There are two accounts of the Creation found in Genesis (JEHN uh suhs), the first book of the Bible. They are not exactly the same, but both of these poetic stories give meaning to a great mystery of life: how the world and people came into being.

The First Creation Story

The first Creation story, found in Genesis 1:1–2:4, teaches us that there is one God and that God is the creator of the world and all living things.

The most important truth that we learn from this first Creation story is that, with the creation of human beings, God established a special relationship with us.

5. Then God said: "Let us make man in our image, after our likeness. Let them have dominion over the fish of the sea, the birds of the air, and the cattle, and over all the wild animals and all the creatures that crawl on the ground."

God created man in his image;
in the divine image he created him;
male and female he created them.

God blessed them, saying: "Be fertile and multiply; fill the earth and subdue it. Have dominion over the fish of the sea, the birds of the air, and all the living things that move on the earth." God also said: "See, I give you every seed-bearing plant all over the earth and every tree that has seed-bearing fruit on it to be your food."

Genesis 1:26–29

6. We are made in the image and likeness of God. God shares with us the power to love, create, and reason. In this story, we learn that God gives us the earth to care for, to use, and to enjoy.

1. What is the message of the second Creation story?
2. What do we call the gift of God's life and loving presence?
3. From what did God create the world?
4. What are the effects of original sin?
5. How did sin come into the world?
6. How does God's grace help us?

Grace Enters the World

(1.) In the second Creation story, we see that God shares God's very life with us. The Scriptures tell us that "the Lord God formed man out of the clay of the ground and blew into his nostrils the breath of life, and so man became a living being" (Genesis 2:7).

(2.) With that first breath of life, God invited all people to share in God's life and love. We call the gift of God's life and loving presence in our lives **grace.** Because we share God's life, we become co-creators with God. We are called to have dominion over the world and subdue it. This means that we are responsible for caring for all that God has created.

How Evil Entered the World

(3.) God created our world and all people out of love, gracing all of creation with goodness. But, as newspapers and television continually make us aware, evil is part of life. How could this happen in the all-good, all-loving world that God created for us?

The existence of evil is one of the great mysteries of life. The Bible does not ignore evil. The author of Genesis was inspired to write a story that shows how evil may have entered our world. You can read this story in Genesis 3:1–24.

In the story, we learn that the first man and woman turned away from the gift of God's love by disobeying God. From this story we learn the important truth that sin was the one thing that God did not create. Sin was the free choice of people. We call this first sin written about in the

(4.) Bible **original sin**. We see the effects of the original sin and all the sins committed since then in the violence of our society, in racism, drug

(5.) abuse, and other evils. The tradition of original sin tells us that sin is part of life because of the selfish actions of people who choose not to love God. The consequences of original sin, or the condition of sin into which we are born, make it necessary for all people, in each generation, to struggle against the reality of sin in the world.

(6.) Through grace, God is with us to help us live good lives and to work to continue the creation of the world according to God's plan.

A Story of Faith and Love

God invites us to a relationship based on love and **faith**. Faith is belief and trust in God. It is a response to God's invitation to share in his life. The story of Abraham (AI bruh ham) is an example of God's call to place our faith in him.

The Lord said to Abram (AI brehm): "Go forth from the land of your kinsfolk and from your

father's house to a land that I will show you. I will make of you a great nation, and I will bless you; I will make your name great, so that you will be a blessing."

. . . Abram took his wife, Sarai, (SAR ee) . . . and all the possessions that they had and they set out for the land of Canaan.

. . . The Lord appeared to Abram and said, 'To your descendants I will give this land.' So Abram built an altar there to the Lord.

Later ▾ Abram said to the Lord, "O Lord God, what good will your gifts be, if I keep on being childless? . . . See, you have given me no offspring. . . ." Then the word of the Lord came to him . . . "Look up at the sky and count the stars, if you can. Just so," he added, "shall your descendants be." Abram put his faith in the Lord. . . .

When Abram was ninety-nine years old, the Lord appeared to him and said, "I am God the Almighty. Walk in my presence and be blameless. Between you and me I will establish my covenant, and I will multiply you exceedingly."

7. . . . God continued to speak to him: "My covenant with you is this: you are to become the father of a host of nations. No longer shall you be called Abram; your name shall be Abraham, for I am making you the father of a host of nations.

. . . I will maintain my covenant with you and your descendants . . . throughout the ages as an everlasting pact, to be your God and the God of your descendants. . . . As for your wife . . . I will bless her and give you a son by her."

Abraham . . . laughed as he said to himself, "Can a child be born to a man who is a hundred years old? Or can Sarah give birth at ninety? . . ." God replied, "Nevertheless, your wife Sarah is to bear you a son, and you shall call him Isaac. I will maintain my covenant with him as an everlasting pact, to be his God and the God of his descendants after him."

Genesis 12:1–7; 15:2–6; 17:1–7, 15–16,19

▾word not directly quoted from the Bible

1. How can we form a relationship with God?
2. How can we know God? (Answers may include studying the Bible, praying, and saying "yes" to God's gifts of grace and faith.)
3. How can we show love for God? (Answers may include praying, praising God, and living together happily.)
4. How can we serve others? (Answers may include helping at home and school.)

God's Covenant with Abraham

Today we call Abraham the father of our faith. Abraham and Sarah had such great faith in God that they willingly journeyed to a strange land. They trusted that God would keep all the promises made to them. Abraham and Sarah came to value their relationship with God above everything else in life.

God established a covenant with Abraham. A covenant is a relationship and an agreement between two parties. God promised that Abraham and his descendants would be God's people forever. As a sign of the covenant, God promised that Abraham and Sarah would have a son, despite their advanced age.

Our Covenant with God

God's covenant with Abraham continues with us today. God wants us to say yes to the gift of grace. We can do this by placing our faith and trust in God. God calls us to believe in the promise of a great nation that would be blessed through Abraham.

2. 3. 4.

> **VOCABULARY**
>
> **Bible:** the book of God's word to us, about God, ourselves, and the world
>
> **grace:** the gift of God's life and loving presence in our lives
>
> **original sin:** the sinful condition into which we are born
>
> **faith:** belief and trust in God

> **THIS IS OUR FAITH HERITAGE**
>
> God is the creator of the world and all living things. We share God's life through the gift of grace. God calls us to respond to the gift of grace by placing our faith and trust in God and by caring for all of creation.

The Servant of the Lord

Mary was a young Jewish girl preparing to marry a man from her own town. We know almost nothing about her life up to this point, except that she was raised to believe in God.

Before she married Joseph, a carpenter in Nazareth (NAZ uh ruhth), God sent a messenger to tell her that she was going to be the mother of God's Son, Jesus. We do not know how Mary felt at that moment. We only know her response: "I am the handmaid of the Lord. May it be done to me according to your word" (Luke 1:38).

With her simple and trusting response, Mary made it possible for God's plan for the world to be furthered. God then sent Jesus to teach us how to live.

Mary was completely open to doing whatever God asked of her. Her relationship with God was based on trust and love. Because she believed that God knew what was best for her, she responded to God by saying yes without understanding what it would mean to be the mother of Jesus.

Mary has many titles. We call her the Immaculate Conception because we believe that she was the only human being ever conceived without original sin. We call her Our Lady of Sorrows because she stood beneath the cross and watched as her son died.

Mother of God is another title that we give to Mary. It was her cousin Elizabeth who first recognized Mary's special role in God's plan for the world. Scripture tells us that she greeted Mary by saying, "Most blessed are you among women, and blessed is the fruit of your womb. And how does this happen to me, that the mother of my Lord should come to me?" (Luke 1:42–43).

We believe that Mary is our mother, too. As Jesus was dying on the cross, Jesus gave us his mother to help us grow in faith. Jesus looked at Mary and the beloved disciple as they stood at the foot of the cross. He said to Mary, "Woman, behold your son." Then Jesus said to the beloved disciple, "Behold, your mother" (John 19:26–27).

We honor Mary as the greatest of all Jesus' disciples by trying to live as she lived. Most importantly, we can turn to Mary to help us live our faith. With Mary as our example, we can work to become a better sign of God's grace by knowing, loving, and serving God and all creation, as she did.

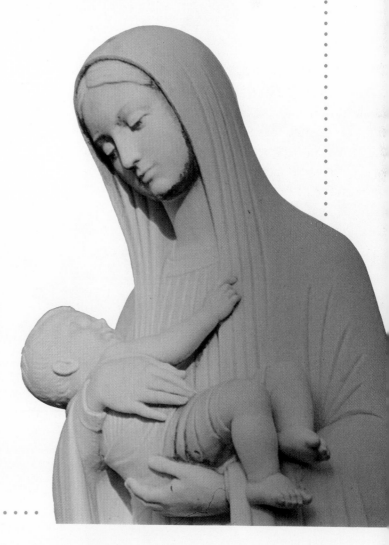

BUILDING OUR RELATIONSHIP WITH GOD

We have learned that in the Bible God speaks to us about God, about ourselves, and about the world. God continues to speak to us today through people, events, and all of nature, just as he spoke to the Israelite people whose story we read in the Hebrew Scriptures.

God's grace helps us grow in relationship with God. It helps us to recognize how we can know, love, and serve God and all of creation. By knowing, loving, and serving God and all of creation, we can take a more active role in carrying out God's plan for the world.

ACTIVITY

Think about your relationship with God. How can you build that relationship? How can you better know, love, and serve God?

I can better know God by _Answers will vary._

Possible answers may include studying the Bible,

attending religion classes, or saying yes to God's

grace and the gift of faith.

I can show my love for God by _Answers may_

include thanking God, trying to live together happily.

_____

I can serve God and all of creation by _____

Answers may include helping at home and school.

_____

The Wonder of Creation

As we look at the world God created for us to use, enjoy, and care for, we see evidence of God's power, wisdom, glory, and love. We are touched by the wonder and mystery of creation.

ACTIVITY

Name something in nature that reminds you of God's power, wisdom, glory, or love. Tell why it reveals something about God to you.

Answers will vary. Possible answers may include:

waterfalls, the Grand Canyon, or a sunset; all the food

God has provided.

_____

_____

_____

Mary's Prayer of Praise

Mary prayed this prayer after Elizabeth recognized that Mary was going to be the mother of Jesus. It expresses her faith and trust in God.

My being proclaims the greatness of
   the Lord,
my spirit finds joy in God my savior.
For he has looked upon his servant
   in all her lowliness;
All ages to come shall call me blessed.
God who is mighty has done great
   things for me,
holy is his name.
His mercy is from age to age to those
   who fear him.
He has shown might with his arm;
   he has confused the proud in their
   inmost thoughts.

He has deposed the mighty from their
   thrones and raised the lowly to
   high places.
The hungry he has given every good
   thing while the rich he has sent
   empty away.
He has upheld Israel his servant,
   ever mindful of his mercy;
Even as he promised our fathers,
   Abraham and his descendants
   forever.

From Luke 1:46–55

ACTIVITY   **Understanding Our Faith**

And God Saw How Good It Was   Using your Bible, skim the first Creation story, found in Genesis 1:1–2:4, to put the statements below in correct sequence. Write the numerals 1–7 in the space provided.

_3_ God created the earth.

_7_ God rested.

_1_ God created light.

_6_ God created human beings.

_2_ God created the sky.

_5_ God created birds.

_4_ God created the stars.

You Said It!   Read over the definitions for the words *grace* and *faith*. Use each word in a sentence to show that you understand their meaning.

Answers will vary. See definitions on page 16.

_____

_____

_____

2

We Follow Jesus

Possible answers: freed

slaves; kept nation together

courage; brought

people together

☀ TOP QUALITY!

What do you admire most about other people your age?

ACTIVITY

Look over the list below. Choose the five things you most admire and write them in order of importance on the lines at the right.

smart	great dresser
friendly	rich
good looking	respectful of others
athletic	fun to be with
popular	honest

1. Answers will vary according to personal preferences.
   _____

2. _____

3. _____

4. _____

5. _____

Abraham Lincoln and Martin Luther King, Jr. have been recognized for their qualities and accomplishments. Beneath the pictures above write what you admire about each of them.

1. How can we describe the crowd's response to Jesus? (Answers may include that the crowd greeted Jesus like a hero or king.)

2. How did people describe Jesus?
3. How might you describe Jesus? (Answers will vary but might include some of the sentiments the people of Israel felt.)

✝ JESUS—THE MOST ADMIRED

One day the people of Jerusalem showed great admiration for Jesus. The following Scripture story tells what happened to Jesus in Jerusalem.

When they drew near Jerusalem and came to Bethphage on the Mount of Olives, Jesus sent two disciples, saying to them, "Go into the village opposite you, and immediately you will find a donkey tethered, and a colt with her. Untie them and bring them here to me.". . . The disciples went and did as Jesus had ordered them. They brought the donkey and her colt and laid their cloaks over them, and he sat upon them. The very large crowd spread their cloaks on the road, while others cut branches from the trees and strewed them on the road. The crowds preceding him and those following kept crying out and saying:

"Hosanna to the Son of David;
blessed is he who comes in the name
of the Lord;
hosanna in the highest."

And when he entered Jerusalem the whole city was shaken and asked, "Who is this?" And the crowds replied, "This is Jesus, the prophet, from Nazareth in Galilee."

Matthew 21:1–2, 6–11

During Jesus' life, his identity was the source of great discussion. His followers called him "teacher" and "Master." They often referred to him as "Rabbi," a Jewish leader and teacher. Others called him a miracle worker and healer. Jesus' enemies thought that he was a trouble-maker who questioned authority and misled the crowds that followed him. During his life, Jesus was both admired and feared. It was only after his death and resurrection that people began to fully understand who Jesus was.

Today, Jesus surely has to be regarded as the most admired person in all of history. In 1988 alone, over 1,619,272,500 people were counted as his followers!

1. What does the word *Messiah* mean?
2. Why do we believe Jesus is the Messiah? (We believe that Jesus brought God's kingdom of love, peace, and justice.)

The Gospels Tell Us Who Jesus Is

In the gospels we read that the people called Jesus the **Messiah**. The Israelites believed that God would send a messiah to save his people and bring about peace and justice. The word *messiah* is a

(1.) Hebrew word meaning "God's anointed one." By the time of Jesus, the Jews had many different ideas about the messiah. Some believed that he would be a great leader like their greatest king; many believed that he would be a military leader with a mighty army who would help them conquer their enemies. There were those who even expected two messiahs. Others were looking

2. for a spirit-filled person that would inspire them. But all of them waited in hope for God's reign of peace and justice.

For us as Christians, it is Jesus who ushers in this period. We believe that he is the long-awaited Messiah. He was not a royal person or great warrior; but surely he was spirit-filled.

3. How do we know Jesus was divine?
4. How do we know that Jesus was human?
5. What is the kingdom of God?

6. Who composed a beautiful poem that described God's kingdom?
7. Name one image in the poem that describes the kingdom. (Youngsters may choose any image.)

Jesus Is Human and Divine

We believe that Jesus is both human and divine. When we say that Jesus is divine, we mean that he is God. Through his life, death, and

(3.) resurrection, Jesus gave us many signs. He cured the sick and gave sight to the blind. During a raging storm that frightened his disciples, he spoke to the sea and the waters became calm. He restored life to his friend Lazarus who was dead. The greatest sign, of course, was that God raised Jesus from the dead as he had promised. All of these miracles reveal that Jesus is the Son of God come to establish the kingdom.

(4.) Jesus shared our humanity. Like us, Jesus had emotions and needs, likes and dislikes. He felt anger, sorrow, happiness, disappointment, and fear. He ate, worked, slept, and cried, as we do. As we read the gospels we discover although Jesus enjoyed being with people, he also felt the need to go by himself to be alone. Jesus was as human as any of us are, yet still God, still divine. This is the deepest mystery of our faith.

We believe that God became human in Jesus. We call this belief the **Incarnation**. The Incarnation is God becoming human in Jesus.

Jesus Came to Establish God's Kingdom

Jesus came into our world to bring about the

(5.) kingdom of God. **The kingdom of God** is the reign of God's peace, love, and justice in the world. Jesus' life shows us the kingdom. He lived the perfect peace, love, and justice that is God's plan for the salvation of all people.

(6.) The prophet Isaiah composed a beautiful poem that described God's kingdom.

He shall judge the poor with justice,
    and decide aright for the land's afflicted. . . .
Justice shall be the band around his waist,
    and faithfulness a belt around his hips.
Then the wolf shall be a guest of the lamb,
    and the leopard shall lie down with the kid;
The calf and the young lion shall browse together,
    with a little child to guide them.
The cow and the bear shall be neighbors,
    together their young shall rest;
. . . There shall be no harm or ruin on all my
    holy mountain;
    for the earth shall be filled with knowledge of
    the Lord, as water covers the sea.

7. *Isaiah 11:4–9*

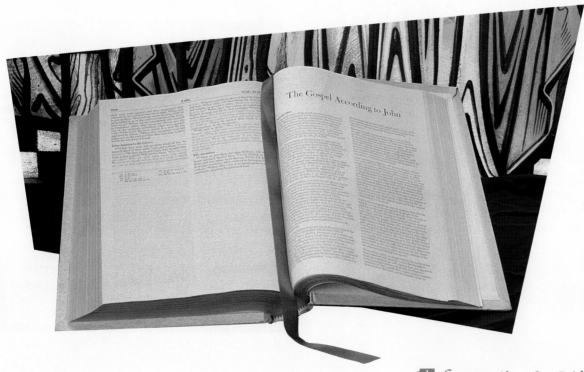

1. How did Jesus treat people?
2. How can we live the new commandment of Jesus?
   (Answers may include loving, caring, forgiving, helping, and respecting others.)

Isaiah spoke of a time when God would be with us, and peace and justice would be seen throughout the world.

As Christians we, too, long for the fulfillment of God's reign — for that time when God's peace and justice will rule our troubled world.

Jesus' life shows us how to live as people of the (1.) kingdom. Jesus treated everyone with love and respect, especially the poor and neglected people of his time. He was forgiving and compassionate. He put the needs of others above his own. He treasured his relationship with his Father and prayed to God often. He promised his followers that if they tried to live as he lived, they would share in his Father's kingdom. Jesus makes this promise to each of us. To help us live like he did, Jesus gave us a new commandment.

Jesus' New Commandment

On the night before he died, Jesus said to his disciples:

This is my commandment: love one another as I love you. No one has greater love than this, to lay down one's life for one's friends. You are my friends if you do what I command you. . . . It was not you who chose me, but I who chose you and appointed you to go and bear fruit that will remain, so that whatever you ask the Father in my name he may give you. This I command you: love one another.

2.

John 15:12–14, 16–17

We call Jesus' commandment the new commandment. It is a commandment based on love. Jesus obeyed and preached all of the commands that God gave to the Jewish people, but with his coming, we can see exactly how they are to be lived out. By living as Jesus showed us we help bring about God's kingdom.

Jesus taught that the kingdom of God is already present in the minds, hearts, and actions of all who change their lives, believe in God, and live with love for one another. He also taught his followers that God's kingdom will one day be completed, and then perfect peace, love, and justice will reign over all the world. Jesus calls us to be a sign of the kingdom already here, and to work for the coming of God's perfected kingdom. We can do this by living as a follower of Jesus.

VOCABULARY

Messiah: the anointed one that God sent to establish the kingdom of love, peace, and justice

Incarnation: the belief that God became human in Jesus

kingdom of God: God's reign of peace, love, and justice

THIS IS OUR FAITH HERITAGE

We believe that through the mystery of the Incarnation, Jesus Christ, God's Son, is both human and divine. We are saved and challenged by Jesus' life, death, and resurrection. Jesus calls us to live according to God's plan to establish peace, love, and justice everywhere.

Sharing God's Love

Vincent lead a comfortable life. His priestly responsibilities were not a burden, for he spent much of his time teaching the children of wealthy parents. Vincent did not seem to mind that his life presented no challenges.

Then one day Vincent was called to the bedside of a poor, dying man. As Vincent prayed the prayers for the dying, he was flooded with memories. He remembered the poverty of his peasant village in the French countryside. He recalled how it felt to be poor, ignored, and looked down upon. That brief moment of God's grace was a turning point in Vincent's life. He decided to dedicate his life to caring for the poor.

With incredible energy and hard work, he reached out to the forgotten elderly of France. He searched the streets for orphans and found homes for them. He worked to change the unjust labor conditions that forced criminals to work as slaves on ships.

He founded an order of priests known as the Vincentians. These men continued Vincent's work of bringing practical help and

Christ's love to the poor. Vincent helped a young widow, Louise de Marillac, begin the Sisters of Charity, a community of nuns who also served the neglected people of France. At that time religious women never left their convents, but Louise took the women who joined her into the streets of the city and into the sickroom.

We honor Vincent de Paul and Louise de Marillac as saints. Their work that began over three hundred years ago continues today. Because of their ability to see Jesus in the poor, schools, orphanages, hospitals, and homes for the elderly were built all over the world. Almost every parish in America has a ''Saint Vincent DePaul Society'' to help the needy.

Vincent frequently told people that at heart he was a mean-spirited man with a terrible temper. He said that God's grace had changed him and helped him to become a loving and caring person. Both Louise and Vincent let God's grace work through them and showed us how to live the new commandment.

LIVING THE NEW COMMANDMENT

We have learned that Jesus asked us to love one another as he has loved us. He calls us to look for ways that we can bring his love to the people we meet.

ACTIVITY

Think of unloving situations or attitudes within your family, with your friends, and within the world that need Jesus' love. Use the chart below to identify the problem you see and how you can change it by living out Jesus' new commandment of love. Look back at the Scripture story (John 15:12–14, 16–17) to help you complete your chart.

Who needs the Law of Love?	What is the problem?	How I can change the problem by living the new commandment.
My Family		
My Friends		
The World		

The Titles of Jesus

In this chapter you have learned that we call Jesus Messiah, Christ, and Son of God. In the New Testament we can find other titles for Jesus. Use your Bible to locate the Scripture passages listed below. List on the lines given with each passage the titles for Jesus that you find.

Luke 9:22. Jesus calls himself the

Son of Man

This means that Jesus was human like us.

John 1:29. John calls Jesus the

Lamb of God

This means that Jesus would sacrifice his life on the cross for us.

Philippians 2:11 After Jesus' resurrection,

his followers called Jesus _____Lord_____

This means that Jesus' followers knew that he was God.

John 10:14. Jesus call himself the

good shepherd

This means that Jesus loves and cares for us.

Which of Jesus' titles means the most to you? Write the title on the lines below and tell why it helps you know who Jesus is.

Answers will vary.

The Lord's Prayer

Jesus taught his followers to pray the Lord's Prayer, which we sometimes call the Our Father. It has been called an outline for prayer because it combines several types of prayer. We begin by praising God and saying his name is holy or hallowed. We pray that God's kingdom of love, justice, and peace will be completed. We ask God to give us the things we really need to be happy. We ask for forgiveness and pray that we will be forgiving, too. We ask God to protect us from temptation and evil. As one of Jesus' disciples, you can learn the Lord's Prayer and pray it often.

Our Father, who art in heaven,
hallowed be thy name;
thy kingdom come;
thy will be done on earth as it is
    in heaven.
Give us this day our daily bread;
and forgive us our trespasses
as we forgive those
who trespass against us;
and lead us not into temptation,
but deliver us from evil.

Amen.

ACTIVITY   **Understanding Our Faith**

You Be the Judge   Read the situations below. Put an **X** beside the ones in which the people are trying to be a sign of the kingdom of God. Identify the kingdom value and write it on the line.   Answers will vary.

_____ Tracy has chores to do at home each week. She does them only after her mother reminds her several times.

_____

X_____ Jamal plans time each week to visit his grandmother.
Possible answer: Love one another

_____

X_____ Nicole calls her friend after an argument at school to make-up.
Possible answer: Bringing peace

_____

_____ Sean spreads a rumor about a classmate.

_____

X_____ Claudia tries to be friendly to everyone in the class.
Possible answers: Bring justice, equality; respecting others

_____

_____ Tim complains whenever things don't go his way.

_____

3

See lesson plans on pages 20T–21T of Teacher Edition.
Circled numbers indicate factual questions; squared numbers are thought or reflective questions.

The Holy Spirit Guides Us

 TEEN ADVISOR

Your local newspaper has started a teen page. One of the features is an advice column in which students from local schools respond to questions that have been sent in.

ACTIVITY

What advice would you give to the students who wrote the letters below?
Write your responses on the lines beneath each letter.

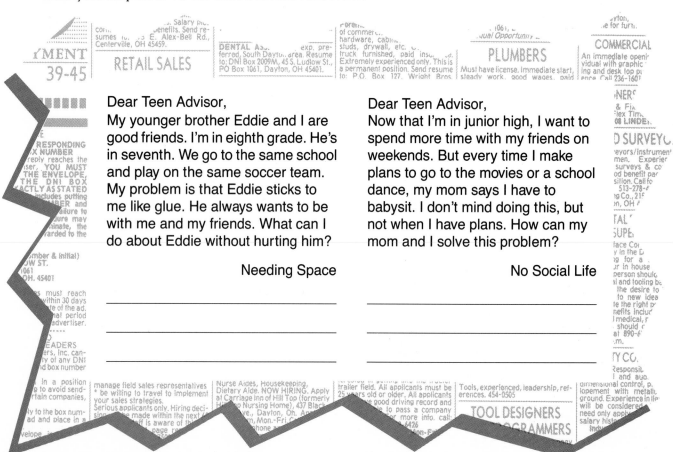

Dear Teen Advisor,
My younger brother Eddie and I are good friends. I'm in eighth grade. He's in seventh. We go to the same school and play on the same soccer team. My problem is that Eddie sticks to me like glue. He always wants to be with me and my friends. What can I do about Eddie without hurting him?

Needing Space

Dear Teen Advisor,
Now that I'm in junior high, I want to spend more time with my friends on weekends. But every time I make plans to go to the movies or a school dance, my mom says I have to babysit. I don't mind doing this, but not when I have plans. How can my mom and I solve this problem?

No Social Life

All of us need to talk to someone about a problem or get advice about what to do about a decision. Whom do you turn to for advice? How does this person help you?

Answers will vary but youngsters may mention parents, siblings, or friends who listen to

them, offer suggestions, and help them make decisions.

1. What was the disciples' mission?
2. Who did Jesus promise to send to help the disciples?
3. How would the Holy Spirit help the disciples?

4. How did Mary and the disciples feel as they waited for the Holy Spirit?
5. How did the Holy Spirit come to Mary and the disciples?

✝ JESUS PROMISES THE SPIRIT

Jesus knew that his disciples would need advice and strength to carry on his work after he left them. Before Jesus returned to his Father, he promised to send the Holy Spirit to help them.
(1.) The disciples' mission was to teach Jesus' message all over the world and to baptize new disciples in
(2.) his name. Jesus said "I will ask the Father, and he will give you another Advocate (AD vuh kuht) to be with you always. . . . The Advocate, the holy Spirit that the Father will send in my name —he will teach you everything and remind you of all that (I) told you" (John 14:16, 26).

Jesus called the Holy Spirit the Advocate, which is from the Greek word *Paraclete* (PAR uh kleet),
(3.) meaning "counselor," because the Holy Spirit would counsel and support the disciples.

The Disciples Wait for the Advocate

After Jesus returned to his Father, the disciples and Mary went back into Jerusalem. There they prayed and shared memories of Jesus while
(4.) waiting for the Holy Spirit to come to them. They needed the Spirit to help them conquer the fear that they would be arrested and put to death like Jesus. They needed the Spirit's strength to help them trust in their ability to carry on Jesus' work, for they had very little experience with public speaking or preaching.

Jesus Sends the Promised One

The Bible records the story of the coming of the Holy Spirit at Pentecost. This was the Jewish festival commemorating God giving the Ten Commandments to Israel. Here is the story:

When the time for Pentecost was fulfilled, they
(5.) were all in one place together. And suddenly there came from the sky a noise like a strong driving wind, and it filled the entire house in which they were. Then there appeared to them tongues as of fire, which parted and came to rest on each one of them. And they were all filled with the holy Spirit and began to speak in different tongues, as the Spirit enabled them to proclaim.

1. How did the Holy Spirit change the disciples?
2. What happened when the disciples taught people about Jesus?
3. What is the Blessed Trinity?
4. What do we remember each time we make the Sign of the Cross?
5. How long has the Holy Spirit been at work in the world?

Now there were devout Jews from every nation under heaven staying in Jerusalem. At this sound, they gathered in a large crowd, but they were confused because each one heard them speaking in his own language. They were astounded, and in amazement they asked, "Are not all these people who are speaking Galileans (gal uh LEE uhns)? Then how does each of us hear them in his own native language?

. . . Then Peter stood up with the Eleven, raised his voice and proclaimed to them . . . . Peter said to them, "Repent and be baptized, every one of you, in the name of Jesus Christ for the forgiveness of your sins; and you will receive the gift of the Holy Spirit."

. . . Those who accepted his message were baptized, and about three thousand persons were added that day.

Acts of the Apostles 2:1–8, 14, 38, 41

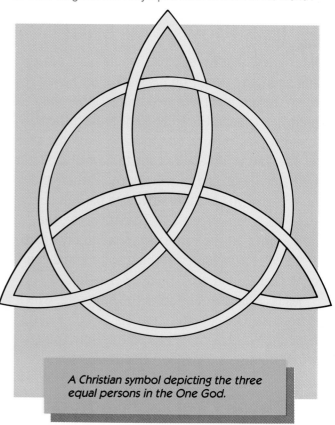

A Christian symbol depicting the three equal persons in the One God.

The Spirit Helps Us Know Jesus

Strengthened by the Holy Spirit, the disciples received the courage to speak convincingly about Jesus' life, death, and resurrection. People heard the truth of their words and the love of Jesus in their voices. They were inspired to change their lives and accept Jesus as their savior.

Jesus' followers recognized him as the Messiah that God had promised. They called Jesus the *Christ,* which means "the anointed one." Because of their belief in Jesus and his teachings, Jesus' followers eventually became known as **Christians**. A Christian is a baptized follower of Jesus.

The Father, Son, and Holy Spirit

There is only one God, yet we know God as three distinct persons. Through creation, God reveals to us one person — our Father, the Creator. Through Jesus, God reveals to us another person — God the Son. The Holy Spirit is the third person in God, our leader and guide.

The union of these three separate and distinct persons — Father, Son, and Holy Spirit — is called the **Blessed Trinity** (TRIHN uh tee). We believe in the Blessed Trinity because of our faith and all that God has revealed to us.

We express our belief in the Blessed Trinity each time we pray. When we make the Sign of the Cross, we say, "In the name of the Father, and of the Son, and of the Holy Spirit. Amen." The word *amen* means "truly" or "So be it!" Whenever we make the Sign of the Cross, we can remember our belief in the Blessed Trinity and thank God for revealing the Father, Son, and Holy Spirit to us.

The Holy Spirit at Work Today

The Holy Spirit has been at work in the world since creation. Under the guidance of the Holy Spirit, the authors of the Bible wrote God's inspired word. The Holy Spirit worked through the disciples, giving them the courage and energy to be Jesus' witnesses and help others believe in him. The Holy Spirit is at work in the Church

6. Where do we see the Holy Spirit's work?
7. When do we receive the Holy Spirit?
8. How is our conscience formed?

9. Who do we turn away from when we sin?

today. God's Spirit leads the Church to be a sign of God's kingdom. The Holy Spirit calls each member of the Church to be loving, peaceful, and just people.

7. We receive the gift of the Holy Spirit at Baptism when we receive the gift of God's life and the promise of his loving presence throughout our life.

The Holy Spirit helps us to live good lives by guiding our **conscience**. Conscience is the ability to judge whether something is right or wrong. The Holy Spirit can help us grow and develop.

8. Our conscience is formed by the good example of our parents and teachers. It is formed when we seek the advice of people who live lives of Christian love and justice. Sometimes these people can be "tough friends" because they help us know the truth. Conscience is formed through the

words of Jesus in the Bible and the teachings of the Church. It is formed by the Holy Spirit, who helps us to live as followers of Jesus.

The Holy Spirit helps us to avoid **sin**. Sin is a free decision to do what we know is wrong and to omit doing what we know is right. It is a conscious choice to turn away from God, Jesus, and the teachings of the Church. The Holy Spirit guides our conscience and helps us know when something is sinful.

9. The Holy Spirit helps us to make good choices when we are tempted to turn away from God, Jesus, and the Church. A **temptation** is an attraction or pressure to do what we know is sinful. A temptation is not a sin. Jesus never sinned, but Jesus was tempted.

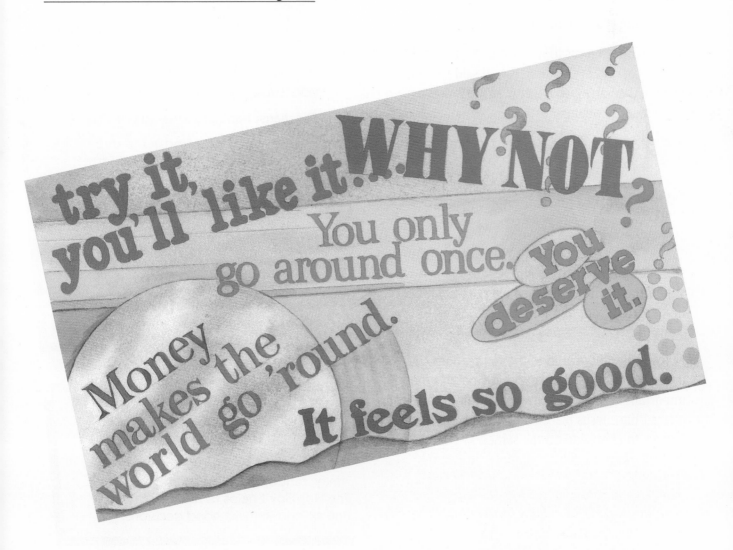

The Temptations of Jesus

Jesus returned from the Jordan and was led by the Spirit into the desert for forty days, to be tempted by the devil. He ate nothing during those days, and when they were over he was hungry. The devil said to him, "If you are the Son of God, command this stone to become bread." Jesus answered him, "It is written, 'One does not live by bread alone.'"

Then he took him up and showed him all the kingdoms of the world in a single instant. The devil said to him, "I shall give to you all this power and their glory; for it has been handed over to me, and I will give it to whomever I wish. All this will be yours, if you worship me." Jesus said to him in reply, "It is written:

'You shall worship the Lord, your God,
   and him alone shall you serve.'"

Then he led Jesus to Jerusalem, made him stand on the parapet of the temple, and said to him, "If you are the Son of God, throw yourself down from here, for it is written:

'He will command his angels concerning you,
   to guard you,'
and:
'With their hands they will support you,
   lest you dash your foot against a stone.'"

Jesus said to him in reply "It also says, 'You shall not put the Lord, your God, to the test.'" When the devil had finished every temptation, he departed from him for a time.

Luke 4:1–5, 7–13

Jesus did not give in to the temptations the devil offered him. He knew that God was more important than all the power and things the devil offered him. Jesus placed God first in his life and asks us to choose to do the same.

The Holy Spirit is with us to help us fight against temptation and sin. The Holy Spirit guides us to know and do what is right and gives us the courage to act on our choices.

God also gives us the Holy Spirit to comfort and help us remember God's love in times of trouble or sadness. The Holy Spirit helps us to respond to God's love by working through us. We can reach out to others who need to feel God's love. With the help of the Holy Spirit, we can care about and serve others so that all people can share in the kingdom of God.

VOCABULARY

Christians: baptized followers of Jesus

Blessed Trinity: one God in the three separate and distinct persons of Father, Son, and Holy Spirit

conscience: our ability to judge whether something is right or wrong

sin: turning away from God by a free decision to do what we know is wrong and to omit to do what we know is right

temptation: an attraction or pressure to do what we know is sinful

THIS IS OUR FAITH HERITAGE

We believe in one God in the three persons of Father, Son, and Holy Spirit. The Holy Spirit is the third person of the Blessed Trinity, sent by God to lead and guide us. The Holy Spirit helps us resist temptation and sin and to make good decisions.

Gifted by the Spirit

Francis de Sales seemed destined to live a privileged life. His family was wealthy and Francis studied in the best schools in France. He earned two law degrees. Everyone thought that Francis would marry a woman from his own class and pursue a career in politics. But this was his father's dream, not Francis'.

Francis wanted to be a priest. His father objected to his decision and tried to persuade Francis to change his mind. Francis was patient and persistent in convincing his father that serving others was his true calling and Francis finally entered the seminary.

After ordination, Francis volunteered to be a missionary in the province of Chablais. His mission was to bring alienated people back to the Church. It was a dangerous assignment, and within a short time, Francis had been insulted and attacked. But Francis persisted. He preached simple sermons filled with practical advice. He was gentle and kind to those who insulted him. To explain why he stressed the positive ways people can follow

Jesus, he told people that "more flies are attracted by a spoonful of honey that by a whole barrel of vinegar." He wrote and distributed small booklets to explain Church teachings and Jesus' love for all people. Soon most of the people in Chablais had joined the Church.

Francis was made a bishop and became even busier. He worked with men preparing for the priesthood and helped them see the importance of acting with humility and love. He trained lay people to teach religion classes. He worked with the poor and encouraged others to serve the poor with their own hands, as Jesus did.

The Holy Spirit gave Francis the gifts of courage, patience, and persistence. We see the Spirit's gifts in Francis' gentle persuasiveness and the encouragement he gave to others who wanted to know how to live the Christian life. We honor Francis de Sales as a saint whose writings and way of life still inspire us to grow in holiness.

St. Francis de Sales helped train lay people to teach religion classes. Many Catholics do this work today under the guidance of the Holy Spirit.

THE GIFTS OF THE HOLY SPIRIT

Over the years, Christians described the ways that the Holy Spirit helped and guided them. They named seven special gifts received from the Spirit. Study the chart below to learn about the gifts of the Holy Spirit. Discuss how we can respond to the Spirit's gifts.

The Gifts of the Holy Spirit	How the Gifts Help Us to Live	Using the Gifts in Our Lives
Wisdom	The Holy Spirit helps us know how God wants us to live.	We grow in wisdom by working to build our relationship with God.
Understanding	The Holy Spirit helps us to be aware of what God has revealed to us through Jesus, the Bible, and the Church.	We grow in understanding by trusting all that God has taught us and by trying to share our faith with others.
Knowledge	The Holy Spirit helps us to know that God is more important than anything else in life.	We grow in knowledge of God by placing God first in our lives and working to form our consciences.
Right Judgment	The Holy Spirit helps us to make good decisions.	We grow in judgment by asking for advice when faced with a hard decision.
Courage	The Holy Spirit helps us to be strong when we have a problem.	We can grow in courage by resisting peer pressure to do what is wrong.
Reverence	The Holy Spirit helps us to love God as our Father and to show our love in prayer.	We grow in reverence by praying to God often, by being thankful for God's gifts, and by respecting God's name.
Wonder and Awe	The Holy Spirit helps us to be filled with wonder and praise for all that God has made.	We grow in wonder and awe by trying to see God in all the people and things that God has created.

Prayer for the Help of the Spirit

Almighty God, adorable Spirit,
Truth, Love, and Light,
Fill my soul with grace.
Enlighten my intellect,
that I may know truth.

Direct my will,
so that I may choose good.
Move my soul,
so that I may completely love you,
the Father, and the Son.

Amen.

ACTIVITY   **Understanding Our Faith**

Triple Jeopardy   Create three fill-in-the-blank questions about what you learned about the Holy Spirit in this chapter. Don't forget to supply the answers. An example follows.

The Holy Spirit came to the disciples on this day. ___What is Pentecost?___

1. ___Questions and answers will vary.___

Question: _____

2. _____

Question: _____

3. _____

Question: _____

Guided by the Spirit   Think of a situation in which a person your age might be graced, helped, or guided by the Holy Spirit. This might be through one of the seven traditional gifts listed above or through another grace given by the Spirit. Write about this situation and the gift on the lines below.

Answers will vary.
_____
_____
_____

See lesson plans on pages 22T–23T of Teacher Edition.
Circled numbers indicate factual questions; squared numbers are thought or reflective questions.

We Belong to the Church

☀ DESCRIBING OUR FAMILIES

ACTIVITY

A Family Opinion Survey

Read the following statements. Decide how you feel about each one. Write **SA** if you strongly agree, **A** if you agree, **U** if you are unsure, **D** if you disagree, and **SD** if you strongly disagree.

_____ Everyone in my family is treated equally.

_____ Our family is more important than any of the individual members.

_____ Everyone in my family has the same amount of responsibility.

_____ Our family should pray together often.

_____ Everyone in my family shares their possessions.

_____ Family decisions should be made by parents.

_____ It is important for our family to eat meals together.

_____ In our family, we show respect for one another.

_____ Love is what holds our family together.

1. In what ways did the first Christians treat one another like a family?

2. How were the first Christians a sign of God's peace? of God's justice?
3. What special work is the Church called to do?

✠ DESCRIBING THE FIRST CHRISTIAN COMMUNITY

In a book called the *Acts of the Apostles* that is found in the New Testament, we find a description of the early Christian community that would easily fit that of a well-knit family.

1. "They devoted themselves to the teaching of the apostles and to the communal life, to the breaking of the bread and to the prayers. . . . All who believed were together and had all things in common; they would sell their property and possessions and divided them among all according to each one's need. Every day they devoted themselves to meeting together in the temple area and to breaking bread in their homes. They ate their meals with exultation and sincerity of heart, praising God and enjoying favor with all people. And every day the Lord added to their number those who were being saved."

Acts of the Apostles 2:42–47

The word *family* is an appropriate description of the first Christian communities. Their sincerity and joyful manner impressed others and attracted new members to the community that Jesus established.

The disciples' teachings helped the growing community understand that they were called to be a sign of God's kingdom in the world. Their love and equal treatment of one another reflected

2. God's love for all people. Their willingness to forgive and cooperate with one another was a sign of God's peace. When they cared for the poor, the sick, and the elderly, they were a sign of God's love for justice.

3. God calls the Church today to be a sign of the kingdom on earth by working together to bring love, peace, and justice to the world. **Justice** is the fair and equal treatment of all persons.

Describing the Church

In the New Testament and in modern Church documents, we find many images or symbols which help us understand what the Church is and how the Church lives out its call to bring about God's kingdom.

(1.) One of the images is that of *The People of God*, a community that is called by God and assembled by Jesus. Through Jesus, God established a new covenant with his followers. The apostle Peter tells us, "You are a chosen race, a royal priesthood, a holy nation, a people of his own, so you may announce the praises" of him who called you out of the darkness into his wonderful light. Once you were 'no people' but now you are God's people . . ." (1 Peter 2:9-10).

As the People of God, we are called to respond to the covenant by continuing Jesus' mission of bringing the kingdom of God to the world.

The Church is sometimes called the *Pilgrim Church*. Like the pilgrims who traveled to our country seeking freedom, we too are on a journey. It is a journey to everlasting life with God. On our journey we often encounter difficulties and suffering. But Jesus and the Holy Spirit are always with us.

It was Saint Paul who first called the Church the *Body of Christ*. He compared the Church to the many parts of the human body. With Christ as the head and all the members of the Church making up the many parts, Paul shows us that we are united as one in Christ's Body. Yet we each make special contributions to build up the Body of Christ. Just as the hand can do things the eye cannot do, each of us is called to use our talents and gifts in whatever way we can to help the Church grow into a better sign of God's kingdom.

The people of the Church are called to be *the light to the world*. By following Jesus, the Light, we can overcome the darkness of sin and death. Jesus wants us to light the way by trying to live as he lived, by giving others a good example, and

2. How can we accomplish the mission of the Church?
3. What is ministry?
4. Name one way you can build your Church community.
5. How can you share God's word?

by reaching out to those who need Jesus' light, which shines through us.

These descriptions help us understand the reality and the mystery of the Church. We are both a sign of the kingdom of God, and a means, or way, of God's kingdom being completed.

Christians Carry On Jesus' Mission

We know that the Church is called to bring about the kingdom of God. We accomplish this mission through ministry. **Ministry** is personal service to others in response to God's call. We are called to four ministries: building community, sharing God's word, worshiping God, and serving others.

The Community of Jesus

When Jesus began his ministry, he invited a small group of people to join him. During the three years of Jesus' ministry, he helped the disciples build a caring and loving community. Later, as they carried out Jesus' mission, they shared with new believers the importance of building a community founded on love for Jesus and one another.

We build community in the Church today by sharing our gifts and talents with others. We can take part in parish activities to build community and get to know everyone. We can welcome new members. We can also participate in this ministry by showing that we care about others.

A Witnessing Community

Jesus asked his disciples to go everywhere in the world to teach the good news. We have learned that the mission of the disciples is our mission too. Like them, we are called to share God's word. Priests and deacons do this in a special way by preaching. Lectors, who read from the Bible at Mass, also have a special role in this ministry.

We can become witnesses to all that God has revealed by letting God's word work through us.

We can share the Scriptures with others and help them understand what God's word means to us.

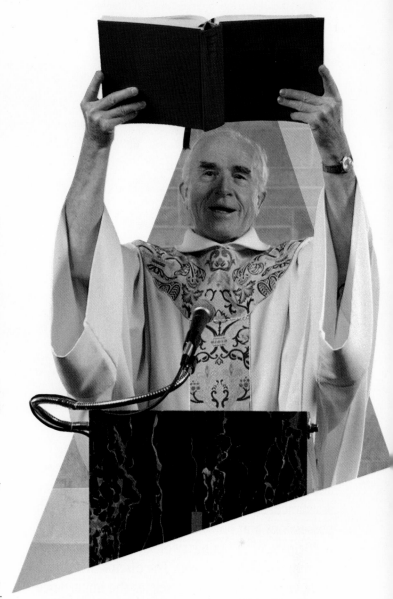

We can ask the Holy Spirit to inspire us when we hear a Scripture story. The Holy Spirit will help us put God's word into practice in our lives and inspire us to be more loving and forgiving at home, at school, and in our community.

A Worshiping Community

We are called to the ministry of **worship**. Worship is giving honor and praise to God. We worship God because of his goodness in creating the world and all living things. We give honor and praise to God because of the great love God has shown and continues to show for all people. The greatest act of worship in the Catholic Church is the Mass, when we gather to share a special meal in memory of Jesus and to re-enact the sacrifice of Calvary.

A Community of Service

Each of us is called to the ministry of service.
1. We serve others by being aware of people's needs
and trying to help the individual. When we offer
assistance, show care and concern, and share our
possessions and ourselves with others, we
participate in the ministry of service. Jesus is our
example of perfect service. The disciple Mark tells
us how Jesus taught the disciples the importance
of service.

"They came to Capernaum and, once inside
the house, he began to ask them, "What were
you arguing about on the way?" But they
remained silent. They had been discussing among
themselves on the way who was the greatest.
Then he (Jesus) sat down, called the Twelve, and
said to them, "If anyone wishes to be first, he
shall be the last of all and the servant of all."

Mark 9:33–35

Jesus wanted his followers to know that all people
are equal before God and that greatness is not
measured by our popularity or the things we have.
2. He taught them that what matters are the things
we have done in the loving service of others.

VOCABULARY

justice: the fair and equal treatment of all persons

ministry: a personal service to others in response to God's call

worship: giving honor and praise to glorify God

THIS IS OUR FAITH HERITAGE

We belong to the Catholic Church. The
Church is called to be a sign of God's
kingdom by working to bring God's love,
peace, and justice to the world. We minister
by building community, sharing God's word,
worshiping God, and serving others.

Our Greatest Missionary

Saul was a Pharisee, a member of a Jewish sect that strictly observed all of the Jewish law and tradition in the greatest detail. He desperately wanted to put an end to the spread of Christianity. He was fanatic in his pursuit of the Christians.

One day on his way to arrest some Christians, a blinding light knocked him to the ground. As he lay there, he heard a voice saying, "Saul, Saul, why are you persecuting me?" Unable to see, Saul demanded to know who was speaking to him. A voice answered, "I am Jesus, whom you are persecuting" (Acts of the Apostles 9:4).

The blind Saul was led into the city of Damascus where he was cared for by Christians. After three days, one of the disciples came and laid his hands on Saul, telling him that Jesus would help him regain his sight and receive the Holy Spirit. At once, Saul's eyesight was restored. He was baptized and began to live the Christian life.

Saul, also known as Paul, began to preach about Jesus. The Jews were outraged that he had become a traitor to their beliefs, and they began to persecute him. Once, they came so close to capturing him that he had to escape by being lowered over the city wall in a basket.

Many people heard Paul's preaching and became Christians. He established many Christian communities in foreign lands. The details of his three long journeys are recorded in the New Testament along with the letters he wrote to these communities. In them we see that Paul reflected on his experience on the road to Damascus and came to realize that the Spirit of Jesus is with each of us. He concluded that we are all one in Christ. This is why Paul began to call the Church the Body of Christ.

Paul worked to bring Gentiles, or non-Jews, into the Christian faith. This was a cause of great concern and debate. Paul answered the objections by reminding everyone that Jesus had come to save all people.

St. Paul was our greatest missionary. He was a man of action who showed us how to live the Christian life. His life is a reminder to us that through ministry we work to bring God's kingdom to the world.

BUILDING UP THE BODY OF CHRIST

We have learned that St. Paul's description of the Church as the Body of Christ is a call to use our talents and gifts to build up Christ's Body, the Church, so that we can become a better sign of God's kingdom in the world.

ACTIVITY

On the lines below, name two talents or gifts that you have. Tell how they can be used to build up the Body of Christ.   Answers will vary.

1. Possible answers might include: using our gifts of
laughter and good humor to make others happy; being

2. friendly to include others and letting them feel God's
love through us.

Identifying the Church's Ministries

Look at the lists of activities that are often done as part of a parish's ministry. Identify the category that each ministry belongs in by placing a check in the correct box. Some activities may be used in more than one category. Then circle the ministry that you would most like to do.

	building community	sharing God's word	worshiping God	serving others
teaching religion	✓	✓		✓
being the parish secretary	✓			✓
working in a soup kitchen	✓			✓
cleaning the church			✓	✓
planning a parish party	✓			✓
ushering			✓	✓
visiting the sick	✓			✓
reading at Mass		✓	✓	
singing in the choir	✓		✓	
being a deacon	✓	✓	✓	✓
running bingo	✓			✓
collecting food for the poor	✓			✓
making banners for church		✓	✓	✓
participating in the blood drive	✓			✓
being in the Christmas pageant	✓	✓	✓	✓
working with teens	✓	✓		✓

Possible answers.

A Prayer of Petition

Prayers of petition are one of four basic ways of worshiping God through prayer. We will study the other forms in later chapters. When we pray a prayer of petition, we place our needs before God. We ask God to be with us and to help us in many ways.

Three prayers of petition about the Church's ministry are found below. Write a fourth petition on the lines provided. In your petition, ask God to help you serve others in some specific way. Then pray the prayer aloud. After each petition, respond, "We minister in your name, Lord."

• Be with us, Lord as we build community. Help us accept others. Give us a spirit of unity, love, and belonging. We pray . . .

• Be with us, Lord as we share your word. Help your word come alive in our hearts so that we may live all that you have taught us. We pray . . .

• Help us to worship you, Lord and give you thanks and praise always. We pray . . .

Our Petition

Answers will vary.
_____

_____

ACTIVITY **Understanding Our Faith**

Like What?   In this chapter, you have learned that many images are used to describe the Church. These descriptions help us know how the Church lives out her calling to be a sign of God's kingdom in the world.
Describe how you think the Church is like each of these images on the lines below.

"People of God" describes the Church well because ___ Possible answers might include that we were chosen
as God's people to continue Jesus' mission.

"Pilgrim people" is an excellent image of the Church because ___ Possible answers might include that we are
on a journey and that we are seeking everlasting life.

"The Body of Christ" shows the diversity of the Church because ___ Possible answers might include that each
member brings his or her gifts to the effort of bringing about God's kingdom of peace, love, and justice.

The Marks of the Church

 ## AN IDENTITY ACROSTIC

Your likes, your dislikes, your family background, your talents, your place in your family, your features and hair color, your feelings, and your interests all say who you are. They are a clue to your identity.

ACTIVITY

Use each letter in the word *Identity* to tell something about who you are. For example, the first "I" in the word could stand for **I**maginative, creat**I**ve, or likes **I**ce cream. Answers will vary.

_____	I	_____
_____	D	_____
_____	E	_____
_____	N	_____
_____	T	_____
_____	I	_____
_____	T	_____
_____	Y	_____

1. What special characteristics impressed the people about the first Christians?
2. Who taught the Church community as it grew?
3. How did the new leaders share in the apostles' work?
4. Why did Saint Paul call those who believed in Jesus "saints"?
5. Who can belong to the Church?
6. Name how the Church expresses her beliefs.

✚ UNMISTAKABLE CHRISTIAN IDENTITY

(1.) "See how these Christians love one another!" This is what the people would say as they observed the followers of Jesus sharing their possessions and caring for one another. The Christian communities had an unmistakable group identity that grew out of their love for Jesus and one another.

Christians Heard the Good News

(2.) The Church grew from a small community taught by Jesus to a larger community taught by the apostles. The word **apostle** means "one who is sent." The apostles were sent by Jesus to preach and teach in his name. They witnessed all that Jesus said and did, and Jesus entrusted his teachings to them. With the guidance of the Holy Spirit, the apostles were able to teach others all that Jesus had taught them. Through them, many people came to believe in Jesus and join the Church.

As the Church grew, the apostles chose other Christians to share in their ministry of teaching the good news of Jesus' life, death, and resurrection. Paul was not one of the original apostles, yet he became a leader of the early (3.) Church because of his missionary activity. Like the apostles, the leaders chosen by them spread God's word and baptized all those who came to believe in Jesus.

Christians Share God's Life

(4.) At Baptism, new believers received God's life. Paul called all those who accepted Jesus Christ "saints" because God's life, that they shared, made them holy. As they listened to the apostles and tried to live as Jesus showed them, they grew in holiness as they became more like God.

Christians Include Everyone

(5.) Through the work of missionaries like Paul, the Church grew worldwide and welcomed people of every race and nationality. The good news was shared with people of every age, economic level, and sex. Paul said, "There is neither Jew nor Greek, . . . slave nor free person, . . . male and female" (Galatians 3:28). Everyone was invited to believe in Jesus and join the Church.

Christians Express Their Beliefs

As the Church grew, it became important to preserve the important teachings and our beliefs about God, Jesus, the Holy Spirit, and the (6.) Church's mission in the world. These beliefs are expressed in the **creeds** of the Church. Creeds are summaries of what we believe as Catholics. The creeds have helped the Church remain faithful to the teachings of Jesus.

✚ *Learning About Our Faith* **45**

The first creeds were in question and answer form and were used during the baptism of new members into the Church. The earliest written creed was probably the Apostles' Creed. Like the earlier creeds it was closely associated with Baptism, but it was also an important part of the daily prayer life of Christians. Begun in 325, the Nicene Creed was completed in 381. The Nicene Creed was added to the formal worship of the Church and prayed at Mass.

(1.) Our creeds express what the Church is called to be. They remind us that the important truths of our faith have been passed down to us from the apostles, who were taught by Jesus and guided by the Holy Spirit.

The Marks of the Church

In the Nicene Creed, we learn that there are four marks or ways to identify the Church. We pray, (2.) "We believe in the one, holy, catholic, and apostolic Church." These marks are signs of our identity as Catholics. Study the chart below to understand the four marks of the Church and how you can live them.

The Marks of the Church	What the Marks Mean	How the Marks Identify Us
The Church is **one.**	We believe in one God, one Savior and Lord, one Holy Spirit, one faith, and one Baptism. Our belief in Jesus unites us.	We worship and pray together. We use our gifts and talents to build unity. The Holy Spirit helps us work together in peace and love.
The Church is **holy.**	The Church is holy as Jesus and the Holy Spirit are holy. God shares holiness with us through grace. The Church calls us to become holy and full of God's goodness.	We become holy through worshiping together, reading the Bible, and praying. These things help us know what God wants for us. We follow Jesus' example of love and forgiveness.
The Church is **catholic.**	The word *catholic* means "universal." The Church is a worldwide community. The Church welcomes people from every race, nation, sex, and social and economic class.	We believe in the equal treatment of all people. We treat everyone with love and respect. We try to see Jesus in all people. We want everyone to share in God's kingdom.
The Church is **apostolic.**	The teachings of Jesus continue on in our world today. The truths of our faith and our way of life have come down to us from the apostles and Church leaders called bishops.	We share the good news of Jesus and live as Jesus has asked us to live. We listen to the teachings of Church leaders, the bishops — who are the successors of the apostles.

Church Leaders

Jesus chose one of those who had been with him from the beginning of his ministry to lead the community he established. This story tells how Jesus gave him the authority to teach God's word.

When Jesus went into the region of Caesarea Philippi he asked his disciples, "Who do people say that the Son of Man is?" They replied, "Some say John the Baptist, others Elijah, still others Jeremiah or one of the prophets." He said to them, "But who do you say that I am?" Simon Peter said in reply, "You are the Messiah, the Son of the living God." Jesus said to him in reply, "Blessed are you Simon son of Jonah. For flesh and blood has not revealed this to you, but my heavenly Father. And so I say to you, you are Peter, and upon this rock I will build my church, and the gates of the netherworld shall not prevail against it. I will give you the keys to the kingdom of heaven."

Matthew 16: 13–19

3. Jesus chose Peter as the leader of his followers. The name Peter means "rock." Jesus told Peter that he was to be the strong foundation on which the Church would be built. Jesus knew that Peter believed that Jesus was the Messiah and that he would share his faith with others. The keys to the kingdom that Jesus promised were a sign that Peter was given the authority to lead and guide the Church.

After Jesus returned to his Father, the Holy Spirit guided Peter in assuming the role of leader and spokesman for the Church. He became the first Bishop of Rome. Those who succeeded, or followed, Peter as the Bishop of Rome are called

4. popes. The **pope** is the leader and chief teacher of the Catholic Church. We believe that the pope represents Jesus on earth and speaks with Jesus' authority on matters of faith. The word *pope* comes from the Latin and Greek words that mean "father." We call the pope the Holy Father.

Pope John Paul II

1. What is the role of the bishops?

2. How do our Church leaders lead us as Jesus did?

VOCABULARY

apostle: one who was sent by Jesus to preach and teach in his name

bishops: those called to carry on the works of the apostles

creeds: summaries of what we believe as Catholics

marks of the Church: four ways to identify the Church

pope: the leader and chief teacher of the Catholic Church

THIS IS OUR FAITH HERITAGE

We believe that four marks identify the Catholic Church. We are called to be one, holy, catholic, and apostolic. The leader of the Catholic Church on earth is the pope. Church leaders help us become a better sign of God's Kingdom.

(1.) **Bishops** carry on the work of the apostles. Like the apostles, the bishops preach, celebrate the sacraments, and serve in Jesus' name. They often lead a diocese, which is a group of Catholic communities called parishes. The bishops also have the responsibility of working in unity with the pope to keep the Church faithful to the teachings of Jesus. The Holy Spirit guides our leaders in this task.

The leaders of our Church are called to lead as Jesus did. Jesus saw himself as a servant and (2.) emphasized service throughout his ministry. The popes and bishops serve the Church and help us become better signs of the one, holy, catholic, and apostolic Church.

A Fisherman Turned Shepherd

Peter was a fisherman who was called to follow Jesus. He had no idea of what Jesus had in store for him.

Jesus chose Peter to lead his followers. To prepare Peter for this responsibility Jesus described a good leader by describing a good shepherd. Peter understood that Jesus was describing his own idea of leadership.

"I am the good shepherd, . . . and I will lay down my life for the sheep. I have other sheep that do not belong to this fold. These also I must lead, . . . and there will be one flock, one shepherd" (John 10:14–16).

Peter was not perfect. Rather he struggled with doubts and fears. Once, when Jesus asked him to walk on water, Peter doubted that Jesus could keep him from drowning. After Jesus' arrest, Peter ran away and lied about knowing him. Three times Peter cowardly denied Jesus. Deeply regretting his denial of Jesus, Peter was greatly sorrowed as he reflected on what he had done.

After the resurrection, Jesus asked Peter if he loved him. Three times, Peter said that he did. In this way, Peter showed his deep sorrow for his triple denial. Jesus said to him, "Tend my lambs; Feed my sheep." These words made the disciple understand that he was truly reconciled to Jesus and that the Lord wanted Peter to shepherd his Church.

Jesus forgave Peter for his doubt and fear. Jesus had confidence in Peter and knew that the Holy Spirit would give him the strength and wisdom he would need to guide the Church.

Peter was the first apostle to preach on Pentecost. He proclaimed his faith in Jesus in one of the most beautiful speeches in the Scriptures. After Pentecost he went about preaching the good news and healing in Jesus' name. Finally he went to Rome, the capital city of the Roman Empire. There many people became followers of Jesus, and Peter was their shepherd.

After some time the Romans began to persecute the Christians and were eager to silence their leader, Peter. They arrested him and condemned him to death by crucifixion. But Peter did not consider himself worthy to die in the same manner as Jesus. Instead he requested that he be hung upside down. But his death did not end Christianity as his enemies hoped. Instead, the Spirit continued to guide the Church through Peter's successors. His leadership provided an example for all those who would shepherd the Catholic Church in the years to come.

Peter's life teaches us that God has given each one of us a special mission. God will not give up on us even when we sin. God's Spirit will continue to work through us, helping us to become the best person that we can be. Peter reminds us to use our talents and gifts to serve the Church.

WE BELONG TO THE CHURCH

Hidden in the word puzzle below are thirteen words that apply to the Catholic Church or tell how Catholics live.

ACTIVITY

The words are written from left to right, from right to left, diagonally, and vertically, and upside-down. Circle as many words as you can find and use them in the sentences below.

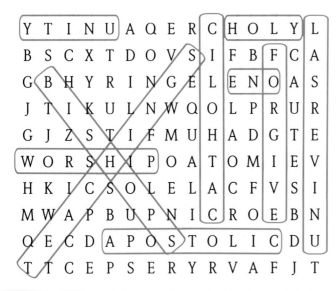

1. The Catholic Church is __one__ , __holy__ , __catholic__ and __apostolic__ .

2. Catholics __worship__ , __love__ . and __forgive__ .

3. Our __bishops__ help us to know the __teachings__ of the Catholic Church.

4. Catholics believe in the __equality__ of all people and welcome everyone to the Church.

5. Our belief in one God, one Lord, one faith, and one Baptism show our __unity__ .

We have learned that Jesus continues to lead the Church through the pope, and bishops. Your parish is led by a pastor. A pastor is a priest who leads the people of the local Church, celebrates with them, and serves them.

Other people are also guided by the Holy Spirit to serve the Church. These people provide leadership through their ministry to the community. Men and women in your parish may serve on a parish council or committee, distribute communion, or teach religion. They may organize activities to help the parish or the people of your city. Guided by the Holy Spirit, they are a sign of the one, holy, catholic, and apostolic Church.

Identifying Leaders   Below list the names of Church leaders in the world and your parish.

The pope of the Catholic Church is __John Paul II__

I live in the diocese of __Answers will vary.__

My bishop is __Answers will vary.__

My parish is __Answers will vary.__

My pastor is __Answers will vary.__

A person who leads through ministry in my parish is __Answers will vary.__

How does this person minister? __Answers will vary.__

__See above.__

Think

What is a Catholic?

What makes us a member of the Church? Baptism

Who leads the Catholic Church? The pope and bishops

What ministries do all God's people share?
Spreading God's word, celebrating the sacraments, and serving others.
A Catholic is a baptized follower of Jesus who under the leadership of the pope and bishops spreads God's word, celebrates the sacraments, and serves others.

The Apostles' Creed

The Apostles' Creed has been prayed by members of our Church for over 1,800 years. St. Augustine encouraged people to pray the creed daily, in the morning and at night.

I believe in God, the Father almighty,
   creator of heaven and earth.

I believe in Jesus Christ, his only Son,
   our Lord.
   He was conceived by the power of
      the Holy Spirit
      and born of the Virgin Mary.
   He suffered under Pontius Pilate,
      was crucified, died, and
      was buried.
   He descended to the dead.
   On the third day he rose again.

He ascended into heaven,
   and is seated at the right hand
      of the Father.
He will come to judge the living and
   the dead.

I believe in the Holy Spirit,
   the holy catholic Church,
   the communion of saints,
   the forgiveness of sins,
   the resurrection of the body,
   and the life everlasting.
                              Amen.

ACTIVITY   **Understanding Our Faith**

Take Note!   Look back over this chapter. Imagine that you are preparing for a test. What facts about the marks of the Church and Church leadership are important for you to remember? Note them on the lines below.

Marks of the Church

Answers will vary but may include: the Church is one because it is united; the Church is holy because it is graced with

God's life; the Church is Catholic because it welcomes all people; the Church is apostolic, we listen to the teachings of the

apostles' successors.

Church Leadership

Answers will vary, but may include: the Pope is our chief teacher and shepherd; the Pope represents Jesus; the pope is

our Holy Father; the bishops are the apostles' successors.

6

Sacraments of Initiation

☀ SIGNS OF CELEBRATION

Everyone loves a celebration! At celebrations we say "yes" to persons or events. Sometimes we celebrate with members of our family. Other times we celebrate with friends or other teammates. A celebration can be planned or spontaneous, formal or informal. Some celebrations are simply a good excuse to get together, like a neighborhood party. Important celebrations have a deeper meaning or significance. We see this deeper meaning in certain signs and in what we say and do.

ACTIVITY

Look at the photographs of important celebrations. Then answer the questions below each one.

Name the signs of a wedding celebration.

ring, promises or vows, expresssions of love

What do the signs mean?

Possible responses may include commitment and family

enrichment.,

Name the signs of a Fourth of July celebration.

fireworks, flags, parade

What do the signs mean?

Possible responses may include freedom and patriotism.

1. What are sacraments?
2. What are the three sacraments of initiation?
3. What is Baptism?

4. What does God give us at Baptism?
5. When are some Baptisms celebrated?

✝ SEVEN SACRED CELEBRATIONS

The Church has seven sacred celebrations called

(1.) **sacraments.** The sacraments are signs that celebrate God's love for us and Jesus' presence in our lives and in the Church. Through the sacraments, we are united with Jesus and share in God's life – grace. We will learn about three of the seven sacraments in this chapter.

We become full members of the Church through the three sacraments of initiation (ihn

(2.) ihsh ee AI shun). The sacraments of initiation are: Baptism, Confirmation, and Eucharist.

BAPTISM

(3.) **Baptism** is a sacrament of welcome into the Christian community that cleanses us of original sin and makes us disciples of Jesus.

(4.) We say a person is reborn at baptism because we believe that we are given new life as children of God. We share in Jesus' life and take on Jesus' work. When an infant is baptized, the parents, godparents, and the Christian community ask God to give their child new life through water and the Holy Spirit.

Parents accept a special responsibility when they ask to have their child baptized. They promise to raise their child in the Catholic faith and to serve as an example to their child by living as disciples of Jesus. To help them fulfill this promise, they choose godparents to assist them in the spiritual development of their child. Godparents serve as an example in living as a follower of Jesus. They also represent the Church community that welcomes the new member. Each member of the community is also a disciple of Jesus. When we are welcomed into the community, we can expect the prayers and support of the other members to help us grow in faith.

Celebrated at the Eucharist

(5.) Baptism is often celebrated on a Sunday, when the Church community gathers to worship God. When we celebrate the Mass, we remember Jesus' death and resurrection. We recall Jesus' promise that we will one day rise to new life, as he did. Through Baptism, we begin to share in Jesus' new life, called grace. When we celebrate Baptism at Mass, all the members of the community are reminded of their own Baptism.

At Baptism we receive the Holy Spirit who is the source of God's life, or grace, within us. The Holy Spirit guides and helps us to live as God's people throughout our lives.

✝ *Learning About Our Faith* **53**

1. What is one of the most important signs of Baptism?
2. What does the water represent?

3. How does the Holy Spirit help us at Confirmation?
4. How can you use your gifts to build up the Body of Christ? (Answers will vary.)
5. What are the signs of Confirmation?

Signs of Baptism

(1.) One of the most important signs of Baptism is water. All living things are dependent on water for life and growth. We use water for cleaning, drinking, cooling, and recreation. But water can also be a symbol of death. We have seen the destructive power of water in floods and swimming accidents. We know that water can destroy.

In the early Church, people were baptized by immersion, or dunking, in a river or deep pool. Being under water was a sign of dying. They went down into the water while the words "I baptize you in the name of the Father, and of the Son, and of the Holy Spirit" were spoken. Then they emerged, or rose, from the water, reborn into a new life with Jesus. This symbolic ritual told them that they die and rise in the waters of Baptism.

This ritual is being restored in the Church (2.) today. The water still represents death and life. We are united with Jesus and share in his dying and rising. But we have our own dying to do: we die to sin and rise to new life with Jesus. We are called to turn away from sin and live a new life, based on the teachings and example of Jesus.

Baptism removes original sin, but the effects of all the evil ever committed in the world are still in our world today. The Church community will help us overcome the effects of war, greed, poverty, and other selfishness. They will help make it possible for us to know Jesus, live Jesus' message, and carry on his mission.

Although water is the primary sign of Baptism, other signs are also used to help us understand this sacrament. Turn to the "Amen" section to learn more about the rite of Baptism.

CONFIRMATION

Our initiation into full membership in the Church continues through the second sacrament of initiation, **Confirmation**. Confirmation strengthens the new life we received at Baptism.

(3.) Through Confirmation, the Holy Spirit helps us to be living witnesses of Jesus in the world. The Spirit gives us the gifts to become actively involved in building up the Body of Christ and carrying out the mission and ministry of the Church on earth. (4.) Another way of putting it is that Confirmation completes or seals our Baptism.

(5.) The signs of Confirmation are the laying on of hands and the anointing with holy oil called chrism (KRIHZ uhm). To lay on hands, the bishop places his hands over those being confirmed and prays that the gift of the Holy Spirit will be strengthened in each person. He anoints them with chrism tracing the sign of the cross on their foreheads. As the bishop, or priest, anoints them, he calls each one by name and says, "Be sealed with the Gift of the Holy Spirit." We accept this anointing by saying, "Amen."When we accept this sign of Jesus, we remember that he is the anointed one, the Messiah. With the help of the Holy Spirit, we will continue Jesus' work to bring about God's kingdom of peace, love, and justice.

6. What do we celebrate at the Eucharist?

7. What did Jesus promise?
8. What do we remember during Mass?

THE EUCHARIST

The most important sign of Jesus' presence in the Church and our lives is the **Eucharist** (YOO kuh ruhst). The Eucharist is the third sacrament of

(6.) initiation. In the Eucharist we celebrate the presence of Jesus' body and blood in the bread and the wine we share at Mass, Jesus' presence in God's word, and Jesus' presence in his community of disciples.

Jesus prepared his followers for this important sign of his presence when he fed a crowd of over 5,000 with only loaves of bread and two fish.

The Bread of Life

Jesus explained the meaning of this event or sign:

". . .you are looking for me not because you saw signs but because you ate the loaves and were filled. Do not work for food that perishes but for the food that endures for eternal life, . . . " "I am the bread of life; whoever comes to me will never hunger, and whoever believes in me will never thirst . . . . I am the living bread that came down from heaven; whoever eats this bread will live forever; and the bread that I will give is my flesh for the life of the world."

John 6:26–27, 35, 51

(7.) Jesus promised his followers that he would give them his own body and blood so that they could live forever. On the night before he died, at the Last Supper, he kept his promise and gave them the gift of the Eucharist.

While they were eating, Jesus took bread, said the blessing, broke it, and giving it to his disciples said, "Take and eat; this is my body." Then he took a cup, gave thanks, and gave it to them, saying, "Drink from it, all of you, for this is my blood of the covenant, which will be shed on behalf of many for the forgiveness of sins."

Matthew 26:26–28

Jesus told his followers, "Do this in memory of me." We honor Jesus' memory each time we celebrate the Eucharist or Mass. The word

(8.) *Eucharist* means "thanksgiving." During Mass, we thank God for all that Jesus said and did. With Jesus we offer to God the Father the sacrificial death of Jesus on the cross. Then Jesus gives himself to us in Holy Communion. The bread and

HERITAGE HIGHLIGHTS

The RCIA

Older children and adults celebrate their initiation into the Church through *The Rite of Christian Initiation of Adults.* This is often called the RCIA. The RCIA is a process in which people hear the word of God, learn about the Catholic faith, reflect and pray, and experience life in the Christian community. Each stage has rituals which are celebrated in the midst of the local faith community. This process is like a journey — a journey of faith. Those who are on this faith journey are accompanied by a sponsor.

We call those who wish to enter the Church catechumens. The word *catechumen* means "one who learns by hearing the good news." The initiation of new members is a cause of great joy to our parish community and also a source of renewal for each of us. We journey with the catechumens, reflecting on our beliefs and re-examining what it means to live as a disciple of Jesus. The catechumens usually receive all three sacraments of initiation at the Easter Vigil on Holy Saturday night. They become full members of the Church.

wine we share still have the appearance of ordinary bread and wine, but through the power of the Holy Spirit, they become Jesus' body and blood. We believe that Jesus is truly present in the Eucharist.

Jesus' body and blood nourish us to become better disciples of Jesus. Jesus gives us himself, the Bread of Life, to enable us to live forever with God. The Eucharist is our spiritual food that gives us the desire and strength to become more like Jesus and to work to build up his Body, the Church.

1. During Mass we recognize Jesus in the bread and wine, as the disciples that met Christ on the road to Emmaus did. We are also called to recognize the real presence of Jesus in others. Through the Eucharist we are called to love and serve others. We hear the word of God calling us to love one another: by caring for the sick, by feeding the hungry, by providing for the widows and children. The word *Mass* means "to be sent." The whole community is sent to make Jesus' presence felt in the world by continuing his caring, healing mission. Christians are sent to bring Jesus' presence into homes, schools, and work places.

Study the Rite of the Mass on pages 98–103.

VOCABULARY

sacraments: signs that celebrate God's love for us and Jesus' presence in our lives and the Church

Baptism: the sacrament by which we are welcomed into the Christian community, cleansed of original sin, and become disciples of Jesus

Confirmation: the sacrament by which we are sealed and strengthened with the gift of the Holy Spirit first received in Baptism and become witnesses of Jesus in the world

Eucharist: the sacrament that celebrates the presence of Jesus' body and blood under the appearance of the bread and wine, Jesus' presence in God's word, and in the community of his disciples.

THIS IS OUR FAITH HERITAGE

The sacraments celebrate God's love and Jesus' presence in our lives and the Church. We become full members of the Church through the sacraments of initiation. The sacraments of initiation are Baptism, Confirmation, and Eucharist.

An American Success Story

Elizabeth Bayley Seton (SEET uhn) was baptized into the Episcopalian Church. She showed her love for God by praying often and reading the Scriptures daily. At eighteen, Elizabeth married a successful businessman named William Seton. She was happy as a wife and mother and enjoyed caring for their five children.

Then William's business failed and he became seriously ill. The Setons decided to go to Italy to stay with friends while William recovered. But after arriving, they were quarantined because of an epidemic. Forced to stay in a damp, abandoned fort, William became weaker, and two days after they were released, he died.

The grief-stricken Elizabeth stayed in Italy with her friends. They were a Catholic family who impressed her with their love for the Blessed Sacrament, the Eucharist. She frequently attended Mass with them and began to ask questions. Elizabeth began to feel that God was calling her to join the Catholic Church. Returning to New York, she decided to become Catholic. Her family was horrified! To them, Catholics were ignorant,

poor foreigners. They turned against her and excluded her from the family. Because Elizabeth had already been baptized, she became a Catholic by making a Profession of Faith. She was 31 years old, a widow with five young children, and penniless.

A perfect opportunity presented itself to Elizabeth! It was suggested that she open a school for Catholic girls in Baltimore. There she would be able to share her faith with young women while providing for her own children.

After a time of struggle, Elizabeth's school became a great success. Women who shared her beliefs joined her in her work. They called her "Mother" because of her leadership and example. Together these women formed the first American order of nuns, the Sisters of Charity. They began schools, hospitals, orphanages, and homes for the elderly and mentally disabled.

We honor Elizabeth Seton (1774 – 1821) as the first American-born saint. Her life inspires us to listen for God's call in our own lives and to dedicate our lives to serving others.

Young woman today follows Elizabeth Seton's example

THE SIGNS OF INITIATION

We have learned that the sacraments of initiation are signs of Jesus' presence in our lives and the Church.

ACTIVITY

Complete the chart below to name the signs of Jesus' presence in each sacrament. Tell what each sign means.

Sacrament	Sign of the Sacrament	What the Sign Means
Baptism	water	rebirth; dying and rising with Jesus
Confirmation	laying on of hands, anointing with chrism	strengthened to live as Jesus' followers
Eucharist	bread and wine	Jesus' presence, our spiritual nourishment

Imagine that you are asked to explain the sacraments of initiation to someone who is not a Catholic. What will you say? What do you think is important for the other person to know? Write your explanation on the lines.

Answers will vary. Possible answers might include:

Baptism welcomes us, cleanses us of original sin, makes

us disciples of Jesus. We receive the Holy Spirit and

God's own life.

Confirmation strengthens us through the gifts of the Holy

Spirit to be witnesses to Jesus in the world.

Eucharist is our thanksgiving prayer of praise to God.

The body and blood nourish us to be better disciples

of Jesus.

Members of Christ's Church should be easily recognized by their actions. How do fully initiated members of Christ's Church act? Name three ways you can show that you have become a full member of the Church through the sacraments of initiation.

1. Answers will vary. Possible answers may include loving and serving others, and working for peace and justice.

2.

3.

Renewal of Baptismal Promises

Leader: Do you reject Satan?

All: I do.

Leader: And all his works?

All: I do.

Leader: And all his empty promises?

All: I do.

Leader: Do you believe in God, the Father almighty, creator of heaven and earth?

All: I do.

Leader: Do you believe in Jesus Christ, his only Son, our Lord, who was born of the Virgin Mary, was crucified, died, and was buried, rose from the dead, and is now seated at the right hand of the Father?

All: I do.

Leader: Do you believe in the Holy Spirit, the holy catholic Church, the communion of saints, the forgiveness of sins, the resurrection of the body, and life everlasting?

All: I do.

All: This is our faith. This is the faith of the Church. We are proud to profess it, in Christ Jesus our Lord.

Rite of Baptism

ACTIVITY   **Understanding Our Faith**

Outlining the Chapter   Look back over this chapter. Complete the outline below.

I. Baptism
  A. We are baptized by ___water___ and ___the Holy Spirit___ .
  B. At Baptism we become _____
  ___a child of God or member of the Church___ .

II. Confirmation
  A. Confirmation strengthens _____
  ___the new life we received at Baptism___ .
  B. The signs of Confirmation are:
    1. ___words: "Be sealed with the___ ___gift of the Holy Spirit."___ .
    2. ___anointing with chrism;___ ___laying on of hands___ .

III. Eucharist
  A. The Eucharist celebrates _____
  ___the presence of Jesus: in his body and___
  ___blood, the word of God, and the___
  ___community.___
  _____ .
  B. The Eucharist calls us to _____
  ___love and serve others___ .

Sacraments of Healing

A CARING INVENTORY

For your information, would you like to rate how caring you are? Read each statement below. Give yourself a score between **1** and **5** for each statement. **1** means you never show care in this way; **5** means you always do.

Answers will vary.

ACTIVITY

____ I am patient with others.

____ I listen carefully when others speak.

____ I am kind to young children.

____ I help out at home without being asked.

____ I respond when someone needs me.

____ I am easy to get along with.

____ I keep my temper under control.

____ I apologize when I am wrong.

____ I respect other people.

____ I help older people.

____ I treat everyone equally.

____ I am sympathetic to people's problems.

____ I pray for others.

____ I am first to make up after a fight.

____ I share my possessions with others.

____ I do not make fun of people.

____ I welcome new students at school.

____ I respect property.

____ I appreciate others' concern for me.

____ I respect myself.

____ I pay attention to the feelings of others.

Total your points to determine your "CQ" —your Caring Quotient. Put your total in the correct square in the scoring box.

Possible Score	Your Score	What It Means
75–100		You are working hard at being a caring person.
50–74		You have a good start but need goals and effort in some areas.
0–49		You have no place to go but up!

1. How did Jesus show care for people?
2. How can we describe Jesus' mission?

3. What do the sacraments of healing celebrate?

✚ THE HEALING MISSION OF JESUS

Jesus showed extraordinary care for all people.
(1.) He cured the sick and forgave sinners. He respected the dignity of each person and treated everyone with love. He reached out to neglected people and was generous with his love. Through Jesus, people came to know God's comfort and mercy. They found healing, hope, and strength
(2.) in his words. Jesus' mission was a healing mission.

His death on the cross and resurrection saved people from sin and death. His teachings and example showed us how to live. He made us one in the Body of Christ, the Church.

Jesus entrusted his healing mission to the disciples. He sent the Holy Spirit to give them the power to cure the sick and forgive sins. Jesus recognized that people would always be in need of his healing and comfort. In his name, his Church would bring God's love and mercy to the world.

Today the Church continues Jesus' healing
(3.) mission in the two **sacraments of healing**. The sacraments of healing — Reconciliation and the Anointing of the Sick — celebrate Jesus' forgiveness and healing.

61

1. What do we celebrate in Reconciliation?
2. How do mortal sins affect our relationship with God and the Church community?

3. How do our sins hurt the Church community?
4. Ask the children to think of ways that sin can hurt them as individuals. (Possible answers may include not being all we can be: less loving, truthful, peaceful, and so on.)

THE SACRAMENT OF RECONCILIATION

1. In the sacrament of **Reconciliation**, or Penance, we celebrate God's mercy and forgiveness for our sins. We have already learned that a sin is a free decision to do what we know is wrong or omit doing what we know is good.

Some sins, such as murder, selling drugs, and adultery, are very serious offenses. We call them
2. **mortal sins**. Mortal sins completely break off our relationship with God and the Church community. Mortal sin is a person's choice to turn away from God, from goodness, and from love. The word mortal means "deadly." We can truly say that mortal sin kills our relationship with God. But through the sacrament of Reconciliation, we can experience a kind of resurrection. Through Jesus' mercy and forgiveness our relationship is restored. We begin a new life.

There are three conditions that make a sin mortal:

- The act must be seriously wrong.
- We must know that the act is seriously wrong.
- We must make a free choice to commit the sin.

Other, less serious offenses are called **venial sins** (VEE nee uhl). Venial sins weaken, but do not completely destroy, our relationship with God and the Church community.

3. Our sins not only offend God, they also hurt the entire community because one of our members has failed in being a sign of God's kingdom. The power of God's love, peace, and justice in the world is diminished through the sinful actions of a baptized member of the community. There is less peace in our families when we are stubborn and angry; there is less love when we speak against another race; there is less justice when we want everything for ourselves. Through the sacrament of Reconciliation, we are reconciled, or reunited, with God and the Church. Then we can begin again to build God's kingdom by doing good.

4.

6. How does God want us to use the gift of free will?

The Parable of the Lost Son

In the parable of the Lost Son, Jesus teaches us that God is always ready to forgive us.

Then he said, "A man had two sons, and the younger son said to his father, Father, give me the share of your estate that should come to me.' So the father divided the property between them. After a few days, the younger son collected all his belongings and set off to a distant country where he squandered his inheritance on a life of dissipation. When he had freely spent everything, a severe famine struck that country, and he found himself in dire need. So he hired himself out to one of the local citizens who sent him to his farm to tend the swine. And he longed to eat his fill of the pods on which the swine fed, but nobody gave him any. Coming to his senses he thought, 'How many of my father's hired workers have more than enough food to eat, but here am I, dying from hunger . . . .' So he got up and went back to his father. While he was still a long way off, his father caught sight of him, and was filled with compassion. He ran to his son, embraced him and kissed him. His son said to him, 'Father, I have sinned against heaven and against you; I no longer deserve to be called your son.' But his father ordered his servants, 'Quickly bring the finest robe and put it on him . . . . Take the fattened calf and slaughter it. Then let us celebrate with a feast, because this son of mine was dead, and has come to life again; he was lost, and has been found.' "

Luke 15: 11–17, 20–24

Parables are stories that help people think about important things in a new way. Jesus used them often to give people a new idea of God. People who think God is stern will be surprised at the outcome of the parable of the lost son. It shows 5. us that <u>God is always merciful and ready to forgive even when we choose to turn away from him by sinning.</u>

This parable also shows us that God gives us the freedom to make our own decisions. This ability is called the gift of free will. God does not control our thoughts or actions. God is like the father in the parable, who knew that his son had made a poor choice in deciding to leave home yet let him learn for himself what was truly important 6. in life. <u>God wants us to use our free will to make good decisions</u> and gives us the Holy Spirit to help and guide us, but we are not forced to choose God's way.

In the parable, we see that it was the son who abandoned his father. The father waited and watched for his son to return. Like the father, God does not abandon or forget about us when we have sinned. God wants us to return through the sacrament of Reconciliation, or Penance.

Jesus teaches us that God will always forgive us when we express sorrow for our sins. God is merciful and welcomes us back with great joy. Then we are reconciled, or reunited, with God and the Christian community.* God does not want us to continue feeling guilty or ashamed when we recognize our sin and ask for forgiveness. God rejoices over every sinner who returns to living as a follower of Jesus.

*You may wish to study the rite of the sacrament of Reconciliation on pages 104–105.

1. What does the Church ask in the Anointing of the Sick?
2. What are the signs of the sacrament of the Anointing of the Sick?

3. How can you express your concern for the elderly and the sick? (Answers will vary. They might include prayer, sending cards, being considerate and patient with the sick.)

THE ANOINTING OF THE SICK

The second sacrament of healing is the **Anointing of the Sick**. In this sacrament, the Church asks Jesus to bring healing, comfort, and strength to those who are seriously ill, elderly, or in danger of death.

Like Reconciliation, the Anointing of the Sick can be celebrated individually or communally.

Individuals are usually anointed at home or in the hospital with family members present. The signs of the sacrament are the laying on of hands and anointing with the oil of the sick. The priest places his hands on the person's head. This gesture is a sign of Christ's presence and healing. He anoints the person's forehead and hands with holy oil, saying

"Through this holy anointing
may the Lord in his love and mercy help you
with the grace of the Holy Spirit."

and

"May the Lord who frees you from sin
save you and raise you up."

The priest prays that Jesus will bring healing, peace, and strength to the sick person. After the anointing, the sick who are able celebrate Reconciliation and receive Jesus in the Eucharist.

The community celebrates with those being anointed as a sign of the Church's love and concern for people who are suffering. As St. Paul said about the Body of Christ, "If [one] part suffers, all the parts suffer with it" (1 Corinthians 12:26).

Communal Anointing

Anointing of the Sick can also be celebrated at a special parish Mass and is called communal anointing. During this celebration, many people are anointed. They may be seriously ill, elderly, preparing for a serious operation, or suffering from a life-long illness.

The body and blood of Christ are our greatest sign of Christ's dying and rising. When we receive the Eucharist in times of serious illness or death, we call the Blessed Sacrament **viaticum** (vi AT ih kuhm). Viaticum means "food for the journey," our journey to everlasting life with God.

Our concern for the elderly, sick, and dying members of our community continues after the celebration of the communal anointing. We are called to visit the sick, pray for them often, and look for ways to be a sign of Jesus' love and care for them.

VOCABULARY

sacraments of healing: Reconciliation and Anointing of the Sick

Reconciliation: the sacrament that celebrates God's mercy and forgiveness

mortal sin: a very serious offense that completely breaks off our relationship with God and the Church community

venial sin: a sin that weakens but does not destroy our relationship with God and the Church community

Anointing of the Sick: the sacrament that brings Jesus' healing, comfort, and strength to those who are seriously ill, elderly, or in danger of death

viaticum: "food for the journey"; the Eucharist received when we are dying

---

THIS IS OUR FAITH HERITAGE

We celebrate Jesus' forgiveness and healing in the sacraments of healing. In Reconciliation we celebrate God's mercy and forgiveness. In the Anointing of the Sick we celebrate Jesus' healing and comfort.

The Forgiving Curé (kyoo RAI)

Perseverance is the best word to describe St. John Vianney (1786-1859). The French Revolution tore his country apart when he was young. It affected even the rural area where John lived. He was unable to go to school and seemed destined to be a sheepherder. Worse, the people of France had to practice their Catholic faith in secret, for those were irreligious times. John's family risked danger by giving sanctuary, or protection, to priests who continued to do God's work.

At nineteen, John decided to become a priest. He quickly fell behind in his studies at the seminary because he did not understand the lectures, which were in Latin. He was dismissed, but he was unwilling to give up his dream. He found a priest who agreed to tutor him, but it was soon obvious that John would never master his studies. The priest went to the bishop and convinced him that John's desire to serve God was all that mattered. The bishop agreed and John was ordained.

John became the curé, or parish priest, of Ars. The people of Ars no longer believed in God or received the sacraments. John wanted to help them return to God. He began to preach every day, wherever he found people. He was like John the Baptist, telling people to repent and be forgiven. In fact, *Baptist* was one of his middle names. At first, the people of Ars tried to get John to leave, but when they saw his holiness and persistence, they listened to him. People began to come to him to celebrate the sacrament of Reconciliation, or Penance.

Soon people from all over France were making pilgrimages to Ars to confess their sins and be counseled by John. The government had to build a special ticket office for the crowds. Ticket agents advised travelers to buy eight-day tickets because the lines of people waiting to see the curé were so long. They estimated that on an average day over 300 visitors received God's forgiveness from John.

John was a failure as a student. This experience of failure in his own life gave John a special sensitivity to the pain of failure in others. It taught him that everyone needs help and encouragement. With the guidance of the Holy Spirit, John was able to help others confess and overcome their own failings in living as a follower of Jesus.

Through the Sacrament of Reconciliation, we can strengthen our resolve to live as disciples of Jesus.

BRINGING GOD'S PEACE TO THE WORLD

We are called to be merciful and loving and to be a sign of God's peace by forgiving others and being peacemakers.

ACTIVITY

Think of a time when you have been a peacemaker. Write about it on the lines below.

Answers will vary. Possible answers may include

stories about apologizing to someone or helping

friends reconcile.

Examining Our Consciences

In the parable of the lost son, we saw that the son, far from home, thought about what he had done. He remembered how well his father's servants were treated. These thoughts may have helped him come to his senses. It is as if he suddenly woke up and saw that he had sinned. This realization led him to quickly return home, sure of forgiveness.

Like the lost son in the parable, we must recognize the times we have sinned by failing to live as one of Jesus' disciples. Reading the Scriptures and listening carefully to them read at Mass helps us to know how to live as Jesus' followers. Examining our conscience helps us to know our sins and what we need to change in our lives in order to be more loving. When we recognize the sinful areas and actions in our lives, we can celebrate the sacrament of Reconciliation and trust in God's mercy and love.

Examine your conscience by asking yourself the following questions:

- How do I show God how much I love him? What needs changing?
- How do I praise and thank God for all that he has given me?
- Do I use God's name with love and respect?
- How do I show love and respect for my parents and others who care for me?
- How do I care for creation? respect all life?
- How do I take care of my body with good health habits?
- Do I fight or argue with others?
- Do I take things that do not belong to me?
- Do I tell lies? gossip?
- Do I cheat? Do I need to change?
- How do I live the Law of Love?

Prayers of Sorrow

We have learned that prayers of petition are one of the four basic ways to worshiping God through prayer. Prayers of sorrow or contrition are another fundamental way of praying. We can pray short prayers of sorrow from the Bible, such as "Let him turn to the Lord for mercy, to our God, who is generous in forgiving" (Isaiah 55:7) or "Answer me, O Lord, for bounteous is your kindness; in your great mercy turn toward me" (Psalm 69:17). We can also pray the traditional prayer that the Church teaches to express our sorrow:

The Act of Contrition

My God,
I am sorry for my sins
    with all my heart.
In choosing to do wrong
and failing to do good,
I have sinned against you
whom I should love above
    all things.
I firmly intend, with your help,
to do penance,
to sin no more,
and to avoid whatever leads me to sin.
Our Saviour Jesus Christ
suffered and died for us.
In his name, my God, have mercy.
Rite of Reconciliation

ACTIVITY   **Understanding Our Faith**

Think about what you have learned in this chapter. Look at each group below. Draw a line through any word that does not belong in the group.

Sacraments of Healing	Reconciliation	Anointing of the Sick
~~Confirmation~~ Reconciliation Anointing of the Sick ~~Eucharist~~ ~~Baptism~~	~~initiation~~ penance ~~viaticum~~ confess forgiveness reunited	laying on of hands holy oil strength comfort healing ~~Pentecost~~

Look back over the parable of the lost son to find images that relate to God. Remember that what we say of the father in this parable, we can say of God. On the lines below write what you feel the father's words and actions tell us about God's relationship with all sinners.

Answers will vary. Possible answers may include: the father's unconditional love of the son; happiness at the boy's return.

_____

_____

See lesson plans on pages 30T–31T of Teacher Edition.

Sacraments of Service

☀ LOOKING TO THE FUTURE

ACTIVITY

Look at the career choices found below. Circle five that interest you.

athlete	politician	lawyer
scientist	veterinarian	astronaut
electrician	artist	teacher
doctor	photographer	mechanic
beautician	architect	priest, nun, brother
police officer	journalist	paramedic
carpenter	social worker	_____
		(other)

Tell why you would like to do this for your life's work.

Answers will vary.

_____

_____

How can being a Catholic Christian make a difference in this profession?

Answers will vary. Possible answers might include ways

_____

of bringing Jesus' values to our everyday activities.

_____

1. What are the two sacraments of service?
2. What does the sacrament of Matrimony celebrate?
3. What is the sign of the sacrament of Matrimony?

✝ OUR CATHOLIC "CAREER"

We have learned that Jesus calls us to be signs of God's kingdom of peace, love, and justice in the world, and to use our gifts and talents to serve others. We recall that Jesus told his disciples that greatness is measured not by how important or popular we are, but by the things we have done in loving service for others.

Today the Church celebrates two special ways that people serve others by sharing their (1.) gifts in the **sacraments of service**. There are two sacraments of service: Matrimony and Holy Orders.

SACRAMENT OF LIFE-LONG LOVE

(2.) The sacrament of **Matrimony** celebrates the life-long love of a man and woman for each other. Matrimony is usually celebrated at a special Mass in the bride's parish. Family, friends, and neighbors of the couple celebrate with the bride and groom. Their presence is a promise of the love and support of the Christian community.

(3.)   The sign of this sacrament is the exchange of promises, or **vows**. A vow is a solemn promise. The bride and groom join hands and promise to be true to each other in good times and in bad, in sickness and in health. Then the bride and groom say, "I will love you and honor you all the days of my life." These promises of faithfulness are a living symbol, or sign, of the covenant that God established with us. The couple's love and faithfulness are meant to be an example of God's love for all people.

After the wedding vows, the bride and groom usually exchange rings. The rings are a sign of their covenant to each other. The priest blesses the rings and prays that they will be a constant reminder of the couple's love and commitment.

Later in the Mass, the couple receives the marriage, or nuptial, blessing. The priest prays, "Lord, grant that as they begin to live this sacrament that they may share with each other the gifts of your love and become one in heart and mind as witnesses to your presence in their marriage." He asks God to bless their union with children and to share everlasting life with them.

At Communion, the couple's union with Jesus will be celebrated as the community receives his body and blood in the Eucharist.

1. How do married couples share their lives?
2. Why can married couples be called cocreators with God?

3. Who helps married couples grow in love?
4. What does the sacrament of Holy Orders celebrate?
5. What are the signs of Holy Orders?

Married Love Grows

1. In Matrimony the couple forms a partnership based on mutual love. Their love grows so that they are able to fully share their lives in an equal partnership rooted in trust, support, forgiveness, and love. This sharing takes place in the everyday events of life and in times of sadness and joy.

God gives married couples a special grace to help their love grow. Through their sexual love, which is the complete giving of themselves to each other, they become one. This is why sexual intercourse is reserved for married couples, who have made a life-long commitment to faithfulness.

2. Through the sacrament of Matrimony, spouses become co-creators with God by bringing human life into the world. When God blesses the union of a married couple with children, they accept the responsibilities and joys of raising their children as members of the Body of Christ. When parents unselfishly share their love and gifts with their offspring, the children can experience and recognize God's own love and forgiveness.

3. The Holy Spirit gives a married couple the grace to grow in love for each other and to work through the good and bad times that are a normal part of living. Yet, we know that some marriages do not succeed. God asks married couples to work together to solve the problems that may threaten their marriage, but some couples experience obstacles they cannot seem to overcome. In these cases after prayer and deliberation, the couple may decide to seek a separation or divorce. Jesus and the Church reach out to the man and woman and their children during these difficult times, helping them to heal their hurts and to remember that God always loves them.

70

HOLY ORDERS

The second sacrament of service is **Holy Orders**. 4. In Holy Orders men are ordained to serve the Church by celebrating the sacraments, preaching God's word, serving those in need, and building a more just community. The word *ordain* means "to set aside." In the sacrament of Holy Orders, bishops, priests, and deacons are set aside to serve the Church in a special way.

Bishops carry on the work of the apostles and serve the Church by leading dioceses, or groups of parishes. When a bishop is ordained, he is given a crozier, which is a shepherd's staff. This symbol recognizes the bishop's role as shepherd, or leader. The bishop cares for the people by exercising his responsiblities to celebrate the sacraments with the Catholic community, to share God's word, to teach what the Church believes, and to serve the needy through works of mercy. The bishop does this by providing Catholic education for children and adults; speaking out for justice; and establishing help for the old, the sick, the homeless, unwed mothers, and many others in need.

Priests are ordained by the bishop to lead the local parish community in celebrating the sacraments. They also preach God's word, help others in need, and help the community grow to become a better sign of God's kingdom of peace, love, and justice.

The word *deacon* comes from a Greek word that means "helper" or "server." The first deacons were chosen by the apostles to care for the needy in the community. As do bishops and priests, deacons baptize, proclaim the gospel at Mass, witness marriages, and preside at funerals. They continue to have a special ministry to the needy as the first deacons did.

Ordaining a Priest

The ordination of a priest takes place at a special Mass. The family and friends who join the celebration represent the community that calls these men to offer their gifts in loving service to the Church. The bishop asks the community if the men are worthy of ordination, and the people can respond by saying, "Thanks be to God," or by applauding.

5. The signs of ordination are the laying on of hands and the prayer of blessing, or consecration. When the bishops lays his hands on the men's heads, he silently prays for the blessing of the Holy Spirit upon them. The bishop then anoints the new priests with holy oil as a sign of their call to serve others.

As the Mass continues, the newly-ordained priests join with the bishop and the community in celebrating the Eucharist for the first time. In Jesus' name, they change the bread and wine into the body and blood of Christ.

1. What are we called to do to build up the Body of Christ?
2. Whom are we really serving when we serve others?

3. What do the corporal and spiritual works of mercy show us how to do? (How to love)
4. How can you serve others using the works of mercy? (Answers will vary.)

We Are Called to Serve

In the sacraments of service, men and women use their gifts and talents in special ways to build up the Church. We celebrate their commitment to serve through the two sacraments of
1. Matrimony and Holy Orders. Yet, all of us are called to the ministry of service. We receive this call at Baptism, when we begin to share in God's life. Jesus taught his followers this story to teach them how to serve others.

"Then the king will say. . . 'Come, you who are blessed by my Father. Inherit the kingdom prepared for you from the foundation of the world. For I was hungry and you gave me food, I was thirsty and you gave me drink, a stranger and you welcomed me, naked and you clothed me, ill and you cared for me, in prison and you visited me.' Then the righteous will answer him and say, 'Lord, when did we see you hungry and feed you, or thirsty and give you drink? When did we see you a stranger and welcome you, or naked and clothe you? When did we see you ill or in prison, and visit you?' And the king will say to them in reply, 'Amen, I say to you, whatever you did for one of these least brothers of mine, you did for me.' "

Matthew 25:34–40

2. Jesus teaches us that when we serve others,
3. we serve him. We call the acts of love described in this gospel account the corporal and spiritual works of mercy. The works of mercy focus on

the basic physical and inner needs of every human being.

The Corporal Works of Mercy

1. Feed the hungry.
2. Give drink to the thirsty.
3. Clothe the naked.
4. Visit those in prison.
5. Shelter the homeless.
6. Visit the sick.
7. Bury the dead.

The Spiritual Works of Mercy

1. Help sinners.
2. Teach the ignorant.
3. Give advice to the doubtful.
4. Comfort those who suffer.
5. Be patient with others.
6. Forgive injuries.
7. Pray for the living and the dead.

4.

VOCABULARY

sacraments of service: Matrimony and Holy Orders

Matrimony: the sacrament that celebrates the life-long love of a man and a woman for each other

vow: a solemn promise

Holy Orders: the sacrament in which men are ordained to serve the Church by celebrating the sacraments, preaching God's word, serving those in need, and building a more just community.

THIS IS OUR FAITH HERITAGE

The Church celebrates two sacraments of service. Matrimony celebrates the life-long love of a man and woman for each other. In Holy Orders men are called to serve the Church by celebrating the sacraments, preaching, helping others, and building a more just community.

The Queen Who Served

Margaret was an English princess. When she was twenty years old, England was invaded and she and her family fled by boat to Hungary. During the voyage, a fierce storm blew their ship off course and it crashed into a rocky shore of Scotland.

News of the disaster quickly reached the Scottish king, Malcolm III. Immediately he offered hospitality to the princess and her family, inviting them to stay at his castle. The grateful family accepted the king's invitation until their boat would be repaired and they could continue on their journey.

The king, however, soon had other plans for the princess. Malcolm fell in love with Margaret. When he asked her to be his queen, he was disappointed that she did not accept his proposal at once. Instead, Margaret asked for time to think over this big decision. Although Margaret realized that she, too, was falling in love, she had always thought that God wanted her to be a nun. Confiding in her mother, she sought her advice; she discussed her dilemma with a priest. After spending time alone in prayer reflecting on God's will

for her, Margaret knew that God was calling her to a life of service as a wife and mother. She accepted Malcolm's proposal, and they were married in the castle.

During their marriage, Margaret and Malcolm grew more deeply in love. God blessed their marriage with eight children whom they loved deeply. Margaret taught them about Jesus and shared her great love of him with them.

Margaret had a great influence on her husband too. As Queen of Scotland, she encouraged Malcolm to educate the Scottish children. Together they worked to set up schools. Knowing that Jesus wanted her to care for the poor and hungry, she brought clothes and food to the people of Scotland. Often she nursed the sick; she even brought the homeless into the castle.

Margaret and Malcolm believed that their love for each other and God was a great gift from God. They shared this gift by serving others through the corporal and spiritual works of mercy.

We can find many ways to serve others, too.

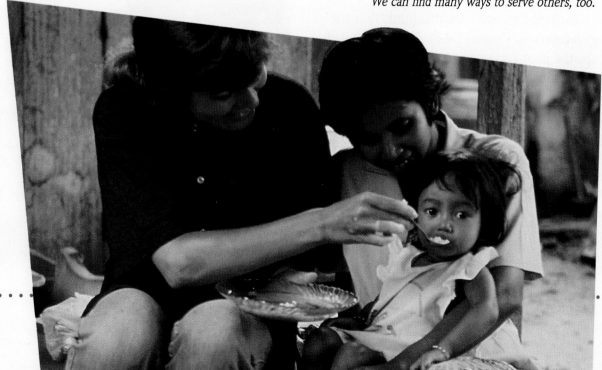

A Servant Church

Name someone you know who has celebrated one of the sacraments of service. This can be a priest, a deacon, or a married couple. On the lines below, write how the person or couple you named has served others by sharing his or her gifts and talents.

ACTIVITY

Answers will vary. Possible answers might include: Father

helps married couples, the poor, and school children;

the Smiths have adopted a six-year-old child to love

and teach how to live.

Doing Works of Mercy

Because of the Church's desire to live the corporal and spiritual works of mercy, many ministries have emerged to address the needs of people.

- Some parishes have established bereavement committees that help parishioners cope with death and grief.
- Many parishes have a ministry of care to visit the sick.
- Ministries to divorced and separated Catholics help people to rebuild shattered lives.
- Another common and essential ministry is the parish-based St. Vincent De Paul Society, which helps the poor and unemployed.
- Parish counselors have become more common in recent years and help parishioners deal with personal problems. Some of these counselors specialize in working with families that are hurt by alcohol or drug abuse.

Find out about a ministry in your parish that works to address one of the works of mercy. Tell what this ministry is and what its ministers do.

Answers will vary.

ACTIVITY

Making Changes   Many of the works of mercy point to major problems in our society today: homelessness, poverty, illiteracy, health care, overcrowded prisons. Choose one of these problems and suggest a way Catholics can work to overcome it.

Answers will vary. Possible answers might include:

people of the community can offer reading classes;

help people make over abandoned homes; write

Congress about health care and prison reform.

Prayers of Adoration and Service

In earlier chapters, we learned that we can pray prayers of petition and contrition. Another basic type of prayer is adoration. Prayers of adoration praise God.

Say to God, "How tremendous are
    your deeds!
. . . Let all on earth worship and
    sing praise to you!"

Psalm 66:3–4

"Lord, you are the living flame,
burning ceaselessly with love!"

Saint John Neumann

Saint John also wrote a prayer about service. As you pray it, think about how you can do the works of mercy.

"God has created me to do Him some definite service. He has committed some work to me which he has not committed to another. I have my mission. I have a part in a great work. I am a link in the chain, a bond of connection between persons. He has not created me for naught. I shall do good. I shall do his work."

ACTIVITY   **Understanding Our Faith**

Getting the Idea   Make a chapter map that plots the main idea, supporting ideas, and details that explain these ideas. Answers will vary.

Main Idea
Sacraments of Service

Possible answers: two special ways people serve others by sharing their gifts — Matrimony,

Holy Orders

Secondary Idea
The sacrament of
Matrimony

Secondary Idea
The sacrament of
Holy Orders

celebrates
the lifelong love of a man and woman
for each other.

celebrates
a person being set aside to serve the Church.

Detail about
Matrimony

mutual love,

exchange of promises

Detail about
Matrimony

having children, co-

creators with God

Detail about
Holy Orders

anointing with oil

Detail about
Holy Orders

laying on of hands

Jesus Teaches Us How to Love

 ## THE STUDENT HANDBOOK

When Mrs. Nelson left the room, everyone began talking at once. "Wow!" said Ric, "This is our chance to really make some changes around here."

"Well, I don't like it a bit," said Anita.

"Everyone will blame us if they don't like this . . . this . . . whatever it is."

Phillip explained, "It's a code of ethics (ETH ihks), Anita. Mrs. Nelson said it's like the Bill of Rights. Basically it's a list of the rights and responsibilities of every student in Creekside Junior High."

"I agree with Anita," added Terry. "The teachers should be in charge of writing this. It's not our job!"

"Yeah? Then whose is it?" demanded Gemma. "We were elected to the student council by our homerooms. Our list is going to be published in the student handbook. The kids trust us. Let's settle down and do it — now!" she said in her loudest cheerleader voice.

"Alright! Let's make this the first item on the list," said Kevin, as he paused dramatically. "Party, party, party!" he roared with a big grin.

Everyone groaned, but Kevin's joke had broken the tension. They started to compose their code of ethics.

ACTIVITY

Working alone or with a group, draw up your own code of ethics for junior high students. List the rights and responsibilities that you think everyone should have.

Rights

1. _Answers will vary. Possible answers might include:_

2. _The rights to be unique, to be respected, to_

3. _disagree with the peer group, and so on._

4. _____

5. _____

Responsibilities

1. _Answers will vary. Possible answers might include:_

2. _The responsibilities to respect others, to see other_

3. _points of view, to be honest, kind, and so on._

4. _____

5. _____

1. How are we called to grow as disciples of Jesus?
2. How did Abraham's descendants respond to the covenant?

3. What are the Ten Commandments?

✝ LIVING AS JESUS SHOWED US

The Church's code of ethics is summed up in our teachings on **morality**. Morality is living and acting in accordance with all that God has revealed through Jesus, the Holy Spirit, and the Church. Through the Church's teachings on morality, we are called to respond to our baptismal call to grow as disciples of Jesus.

God Renews the Covenant

We have learned that God first established a covenant with people through Abraham (AI bruh ham) and Sarah. But their descendants did not always live as God's people. Time after time, they broke the covenant by sinning as individuals and as a community. God recognized that the people needed definite guides or commandments for living morally. But before they were given these commandments, they received a powerful sign of God's love.

In Exodus (EHK suhd uhs), the second book of the Bible, we learn that the Israelite people had been enslaved by the Egyptians and were being

treated harshly by the pharaoh (phai roh), or ruler. God heard the cries of the people for freedom and justice. Responding by sending Moses, an Israelite who had been raised by the pharaoh's daughter, God lead the Israelites to freedom. You can read the entire story of Moses in Exodus: 1–20.

Moses was afraid the Israelites would not believe that God had chosen him as their leader. But God promised to be with him and instructed Moses to tell his people that **Yahweh** (YAH wai) had sent him. *Yahweh* is one of the Hebrew names for God, which means "I am who am." This name points to God's mystery and creative power.

Moses did everything that God asked him to do. After a great struggle with pharaoh, the Israelites were finally set free. They began a long journey into the desert and finally reached the mountain where God had first called Moses. There God spoke to Moses again.

". . . Tell the Israelites: You have seen for yourselves how I treated the Egyptians and how I bore you up on eagle wings and brought you here to myself. Therefore, if you hearken to my voice and keep my covenant, you shall be my special possession . . . . You shall be to me a kingdom of priests, a holy nation . . . ." So Moses . . . set before them all that the Lord had ordered him to tell them, the people answered all together, "Everything the Lord has said, we will do."

Exodus 19:4–8

A few days later, God gave Moses the **Ten Commandments**, which explained how the Israelites were to live out their covenant with God by practicing the laws of love. The Ten Commandments are an important part of the Church's moral teachings. They are guides for living with respect, peace, and happiness with God and all people. The Ten Commandments and how we are called to live them are listed on the following chart.

The Ten Commandments (Exodus 20:2–17)	Living the Ten Commandments
1. I, the Lord, am your God. You shall not have other beside me.	We believe in God and place God first in our lives. We love God more than anyone or anything else in life.
2. You shall not take the name of the Lord, your God, in vain.	We use the names of God and Jesus with respect and love. We never say God or Jesus' names in anger or carelessly.
3. Remember to keep holy the sabbath day.	We worship God by celebrating the Eucharist together on Sunday. We never miss Mass without a serious reason. We put aside all unnecessary work on Sunday to praise and honor God for all our gifts.
4. Honor your father and mother.	We love, respect, and obey our parents and all in authority. We promise to care for our aging parents.
5. You shall not kill.	We respect God's gift of life by caring for our bodies. We do not drink alcohol or use drugs. We care about other people's right to life, especially the unborn, the elderly, the poor, and the prisoner.
6. You shall not commit adultery.	We use the gift of sexuality with respect. We are modest in how we dress, act, and speak. We avoid any persons or situations that might tempt us to commit a sexual sin.
7. You shall not steal.	We respect the property of others. We never take things that do not belong to us. We ask permission before borrowing things and we use others' things with care. We never cheat.
8. You shall not bear false witness against your neighbor.	We are truthful and honest. We keep our promises and never tell lies or spread rumors about others.
9. You shall not covet your neighbor's wife.	We respect the promises that married couples have made to each other. We work to overcome those sexual thoughts and desires that might lead us to sin.
10. You shall not covet anything that belongs to your neighbor.	We are satisfied with what we have. We are not jealous of others' good fortune or success. We are not greedy.

1. What do the first three commandments tell us?
2. What do the other seven commandments teach?
3. What is the Great Commandment?

4. What does the Great Commandment tell us?
5. Who ignored the man lying by the road?
6. How did the Samaritan help the man?

1. The first three commandments tell us how we can love and serve God. They are a call to love, worship, and respect God above everything and everyone else in life. **2.** The other seven commandments teach us how we can love and serve our neighbors and ourselves. They are a call to show love through respect, honesty, truth, modesty, and chastity. **Chastity** is a virtue, or spiritual power, that helps us to use our sexual gifts in accordance with God's law.

The Great Commandment

Jesus fulfilled and lived the Ten Commandments. He summed up the Ten Commandments for his followers. This summary is called the Great **3.** Commandment: "You shall love the Lord, your God, with all your heart, with all your being, with all your strength, and with all your mind, and your neighbor as yourself" (Luke 10:27).

4. The Great Commandment tells us that God's laws are based on love of God, love of ourselves, and of our neighbor.

While Jesus was teaching his followers the Great Commandment, a man in the crowd asked him, "Who is my neighbor?"

Jesus told this parable:

"A man fell victim to robbers as he went down from Jerusalem to Jericho. They stripped and beat **5.** him and went off leaving him half-dead. A priest happened to be going down that road, but when he saw him, he passed on the opposite side. Likewise a Levite came to the place, and when he saw him, he passed by on the opposite side. **6.** But a Samaritan (suh MAR uht uhn) traveler who came upon him was moved by compassion at the sight. He approached the victim, poured oil and wine over his wounds and bandaged them. Then

1. How can you live the Great Commandment?
2. Name the two kinds of sin.
3. What do social sins prevent?

4. How do the moral teachings of Jesus and the Church help us?

he lifted him up on his own animal, took him to an inn and cared for him. The next day he took out two silver coins and gave them to the innkeeper with the instruction, Take care of him. If you spend more than what I have given you, I shall repay you on my way back.' 'Which of these three, in your opinion, was neighbor to the robbers' victim?' The man answered, 'The one who treated him with mercy.' Jesus said to him, 'Go and do likewise.' "

Luke 10: 30–37

In the parable of the Good Samaritan, Jesus teaches us that our neighbor is anyone who needs our help and care, especially the helpless and neglected people in our society. When we fail to help and care for our neighbor, we ignore Jesus' command. The Great Commandment teaches us it is in loving others that we show our love for God. The Church and all of her members are called to be good samaritans in today's world. We live the Great Commandment by following Jesus' examples of love and care for all people. This is the strongest sign of our love for God.

Sins Against Our Neighbor

Refusing to show love for our neighbor is a sin. We have learned that mortal sins are very serious sins which break our relationship with God and that venial sins are less serious sins which weaken our relationship with God. These sins, which we ourselves commit are called **personal sins**. They have social consequences. When we tell a lie, we usually hurt someone else or weaken the trust others place in us. When we abuse God's name by cursing, we lessen the respect others feel for God. When we use harmful drugs, we often influence others to join us. Our ability to make decisions is impaired, and we may be tempted to commit other sins that prevent us from being a sign of God's kingdom in the world.

Other sins, called **social sins**, are committed by the entire people of God. Social sins prevent God's kingdom of peace, love, and justice from

coming into the world. Racism, not paying just wages, ignoring the homeless, abortion, fighting unjust wars, sexism, and prejudice in any form are all social sins. Through the Great Commandment we are called to work to change the unjust situations that allow social sins to exist. We do this by working together as a Church and by working as individuals to change hearts and create laws to bring peace, love, and justice to the world. We can get involved in efforts to make everyone aware of the injustice we see.

The great moral teachings of Jesus and the Church help us make good decisions about how we want to live. The Holy Spirit is always with us to help us choose the good and right things to do. We can ask for the Spirit's guidance through prayer. Sometimes we receive this guidance through others and we must be open to those who offer it to us. Our moral decisions reflect our desire to grow as Jesus' disciples and bring God's kingdom of peace, love, and justice into the world.

VOCABULARY

morality: living and acting in accordance with all that God has revealed through Jesus, the Holy Spirit, and the Church

Yahweh: the Hebrew name for God, which means "I am who am"

The Ten Commandments: guides for living with God and all people

chastity: a virtue, or spiritual power, that helps us to know and to use our sexual gifts in accordance with God's law

THIS IS OUR FAITH HERITAGE

We are called to grow in holiness through the Church's teachings on morality. The Ten Commandments and the Great Commandment are moral guidelines that tell us how we can show love for God, ourselves, and our neighbor.

Sinner Turned Saint

Would it surprise you to know that one of the greatest saints and doctors of the Church was once best known as a very well-educated sinner? Augustine was born in North Africa. His mother, Monica, taught him to live the Christian life, but he showed no interest in living as a follower of Jesus. In spite of Monica's prayers and example, Augustine was never baptized.

Augustine led a wild life. He was a thief, drank heavily, and rebelled against his mother. He lived with a woman and would not marry her even after their son was born. Yet he did not find peace and happiness in any of these pursuits.

Augustine was well educated and taught speech in Rome. He became interested in philosophy and joined a movement that disputed the teachings of the Church. In examining these ideas, he hoped to find the answers he sought, but when he met with the leaders of the Christians, he was disappointed in their inability to defend their claims.

Sometime later, Augustine became a professor in Milan. Out of curiosity, he attended church to listen to the sermons of St. Ambrose, the famous bishop of Milan. Ambrose's words touched Augustine and he began to read the Scriptures. He wanted to become a follower of Jesus but still doubted that he had the fortitude (courage) and temperance (self-control) to change his life.

During this time of inner struggle, he prayed and read the Bible. One day the words of St. Paul seemed as if they were written for him alone. They told him to believe in Jesus and give up his sinful ways. He knew then that God would give him the courage and self-control to become a Christian. He ran to tell his mother, who had been praying for his conversion all those years.

After Augustine was baptized, he returned to Africa. He sold his possessions, lived a life of prayer, and became known for his holiness. Augustine applied all of his talents toward working for the Church. He used his knowledge of philosophy and skills in writing and speaking to teach about God. He became the most famous teacher of his time. That is why we call him a Doctor of the Church.

Eventually Augustine became a priest and then a bishop. He wrote about his inner struggle to find God in a famous book called *Confessions*. His writings continue to give direction to the Church today. We honor Augustine as a saint because of the great contributions he made to our understanding of God and also because his life (354 – 430) shows us that we can overcome our sins and live a moral life as sons and daughters of God.

Some writings of Saint Augustine

Christian Instruction
THE CITY OF GOD
On the Trinity
SELECTED SERMONS
LETTERS
The Confessions
Of True Religion
ON FREE WILL
THE SPIRIT AND THE LETTER
On Nature and Grace
Homilies on the Gospel of John

MAKING MORAL DECISIONS

Jesus calls us to make good moral decisions based on his teachings and example. He asks us to use our intellect and the guidance of the Holy Spirit when we have a decision to make. As followers of Jesus, we need to make conscious, informed decisions for ourselves, even when it seems easier to go along with the group or to let others decide for us. In making a good moral decision, we seek the greatest truth — the answer that will bring the greatest peace, love, and justice. We can make good moral choices by using a five-step process.

1. Identify the decision that needs to be made. Tell all that you know about it. What do you need to decide?

2. Consider possible options. What choices can you make?

3. Evaluate the consequences of the options. How will your choice affect you and others?

4. Reflect and pray. Who are the wise persons you need to talk to? How does this decision show that you are a follower of Jesus?

5. Decide what you will do. What choice will you make?

4. Reflect: _____

_____

5. Decide: _____

_____

Working for God's Kingdom

With your group, name a social sin that you are aware of in the world. On the lines below write what can be done to change or eliminate this sin.

Answers will vary. Topics may include the horrors of war,

neglect of the poor, racism, disrespect for the aged.

_____

_____

A Vietnam veteran remembers the human sacrifices of war.

ACTIVITY

Think of a moral decision that a person of your age might be faced with. Use the decision-making process to make an informed decision.

1. Identify the decision: Answers will vary. _____

_____

2. Consider the options: _____

_____

3. Evaluate the consequences: _____

_____

We Give You Thanks

The fourth basic type of prayer is thanksgiving. When we pray a prayer of thanksgiving, we express gratitude to God for the many gifts he has given us. The Book of Psalms is filled with prayers and songs of gratitude. Psalm 138 is called the "Hymn of a Grateful Heart."

I will give thanks to you, O Lord, with all my heart . . .
I will worship at your holy temple and give thanks to your name,
Because of your kindness and truth; for you have made great above all
    things your name and your promise.
When I called, you answered me; you built up strength within me.

Psalm 138:1–3

ACTIVITY   Understanding Our Faith

Charting it out!   Look at the list of personal sins below. Opposite each sin is the virtue needed to overcome it. List the commandment that helps you practice the virtue and overcome the sin.

Personal Sins	Commandment	Virtue
seeing an R-rated film	6,9	prudence (making wise decisions)
taking drugs	5	prudence or temperance
cheating on a test	7	justice
missing Mass on Sunday	3	faith or charity (love)
telling lies	8	fortitude or charity
disobeying parents	4	charity, temperance
cursing	2	temperance, charity, prudence
being envious	10	charity, temperance
ridiculing another person	5	justice, love

See lesson plans on pages 34T–35T of Teacher Edition.

We Live for God's Kingdom

 OVERCOMING FEAR

Recently a group of twelve- and thirteen-year-olds were asked to list their concerns or fears about life. Their responses are listed below, although not in their order of importance.

ACTIVITY

Look at the concerns the young people identified. Rank your own feelings on the scale for each.   Answers will vary.

Not Concerned	Concerned	Very Concerned

Getting bad grades

Nuclear war

Being poor

Not having friends

Getting in trouble

Divorce

How do you feel about these concerns or fears? What or who helps you to overcome these feelings? Write your answer below.

Possible answers may include talking to parents or

friends, keeping busy, ignoring fears, or praying.

✝ Jesus Brings Us Hope

We know that Jesus cares about us and all that concerns us. Jesus responds to our fears and worries by offering us hope. **Hope** is the belief and trust in all that God has promised through Jesus and the Church. One of Jesus' greatest promises to us is that we will live happily with God forever.

A whole set of Jesus' promises that focus on our happiness here on earth can be found in the biblical account of the "Sermon on the Mount." There Jesus describes how the people of God, the people of the kingdom, should think and act and he announces the reward for those who live the kingdom values.

Jesus teaches us to value the things that matter most in life: love of God, love of ourselves, and love of neighbor. The Beatitudes tell us how to respond to the concerns of others and the problems of poverty, injustice, and oppression that prevent the rule of God's kingdom from being enjoyed by all people in the world. Study the chart on the next page to understand how you can live the Beatitudes.

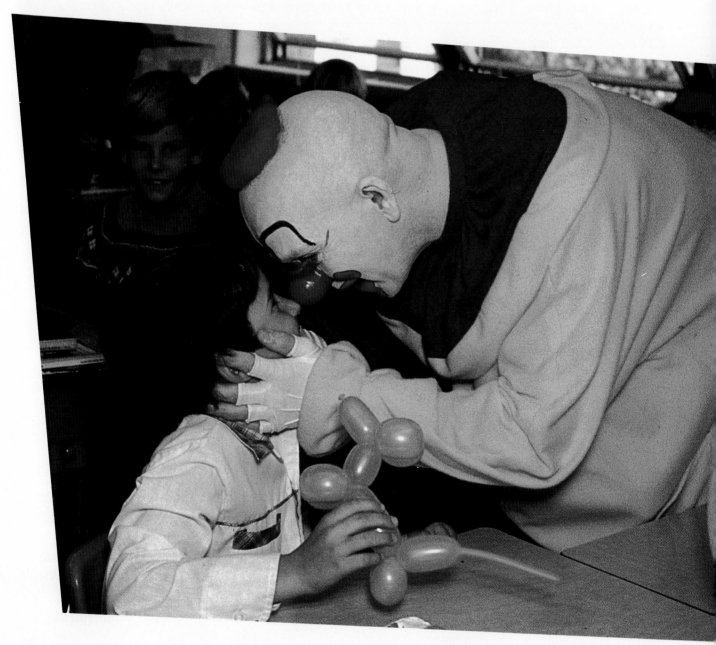

1. To whom does the kingdom of God belong?

2. What do we believe about God's kingdom?
3. What will Jesus announce when he comes in glory?
4. What does God call us to do?

The Beatitudes (Matthew 5:1–10)	Living the Beatitudes
Blessed are the poor in spirit, for theirs is the kingdom of heaven.	We recognize our need for God. We depend on God. The poor in spirit know that God is more important than anything else in life.
Blessed are they who mourn, for they will be comforted.	We mourn the sin and suffering that we see in the world. We trust that God comforts anyone who suffers from loss of injustice. We reach out to anyone who needs to be comforted.
Blessed are the meek, for they will inherit the land.	We humbly recognize that all our gifts and talents come from God. We share these gifts with kindness and patience to serve God and others.
Blessed are they who hunger and thirst for righteousness, for they will be satisfied.	We long for God's peace, love, and justice to rule in the world. We work for equality and truth. We share our possessions with those in need.
Blessed are the merciful, for they will be shown mercy.	We forgive anyone who has hurt us. We accept others and have compassion for them.
Blessed are the clean of heart, for they will see God.	We want only to do God's will and to follow God's commands. We keep our minds and hearts focused on God, seeking good and avoiding evil.
Blessed are the peacemakers, for they will be called children of God.	We work to be a sign for others of God's forgiveness. We pray for peace and unity in our family, in the community, and in the world. We try to settle arguments and disputes.
Blessed are they who are persecuted for the sake of righteousness, for theirs is the kingdom of heaven.	We continue Jesus' mission in the world. We speak out against situations which prevent the rule of God's peace, love, and justice. We stand up for our beliefs even if we are made fun of or criticized.

The Fulfillment of the Kingdom

1. Jesus teaches us that the kingdom, or reign, of God belongs to all humble, kind, peaceful, and compassionate people. God will welcome all those who have worked for unity, equality, and justice to the kingdom. People who have tried to be a sign of God's kingdom by trusting and accepting God's will for the world will share in the kingdom.

We have learned that the kingdom of God is already present in the minds and hearts of all those who live as faithful disciples of Jesus. The kingdom is present wherever God's justice, peace, and love are lived. When we live the Beatitudes, we are 2. helping God's kingdom grow in the world. We believe that God's kingdom one day will be completed, or fulfilled. On this wonderful day,

Who will be a 'Good Samaritan?'

5. Who will share in God's kingdom?
6. What helps does God gives us to live as kingdom people?
7. Who is included in the communion of saints?

have tried to live as disciples of Jesus, we will share in God's kingdom. Those who have not tried to show love for God and their neighbor, or who did not ask God to forgive them for a mortal sin, will be separated from God and the people of the kingdom. We call **hell** an everlasting separation from God and all those who love God.

God Helps us to Live as People of the Kingdom

God wants to welcome everyone to unending happiness in heaven. God gives us many helps to
(6.) live as people of the kingdom. We have the teachings and example of our Savior, Jesus Christ. The Holy Spirit gives us gifts that help us live as followers of Jesus. The Spirit guides our conscience to help us resist temptation and make good decisions. The Church helps us to grow in holiness. Through the sacraments we experience Jesus' presence and share in God's life —grace. The Ten Commandments, the Commandment of Love, the Great Commandment, the works of mercy, and the Beatitudes show us how to live happy, loving lives.

We also have the example of the saints, those holy men and women who have shown us how Jesus' teachings can be put into practice in everyday life. Through the gift of grace at Baptism,
(7.) we share in the **communion of saints**. The communion of saints is the entire community of God's people, whether living or dead. It includes all those who are in heaven, all those who are living as God's people on earth, and those who are dead and still waiting in purgatory to be fully united with God. The communion of saints is the Body of Christ. We help and support one another. We can turn to the saints in heaven to know how to live as followers of Jesus. We pray for those who have died and are waiting to be united with God. We continue, here on earth, to work for the fulfillment of God's kingdom, when the communion of saints will be joined together, body and soul.

(3.) we believe that Jesus will come again in glory. He will return to us to announce that perfect peace, love, and justice rule the world.

We pray for the fulfillment of God's kingdom. We long for an end to poverty, suffering, and injustice. We look forward to a world that does not suffer from sin or sickness. We want all people to live together in peace and love. But God does not want us to merely watch and wait for the
(4.) coming of the fullness of the kingdom. God calls us, as individuals and as the Church, to work to bring peace, love, and justice to the world now.
(5.) Jesus promises great rewards to those who live the Beatitudes and work for the coming of God's kingdom. He tells us that his followers will have the treasures of **heaven**. Heaven is unending happiness with God and with all who love God and one another. God's love for us is so great that we are invited to share everlasting life with God.

When we die, we will be judged on how well we have loved God, ourselves, and others. God will judge us with compassion and justice. If we

1. What is the source of our hope?

2. How can we work for the coming of the kingdom? (Possible answers may include living as Jesus taught, obeying the commandments, and working for peace, love, and justice.)

Trusting in God's Promises

(1.) God promises us the resurrection of our bodies and life everlasting. These promises, made good by Jesus' life, death, and resurrection, are the source of our hope. They fill us with joy and inspire us to work for the coming of the kingdom when all God's promises will be fulfilled.

During the Mass, the priest prays a special prayer after the Our Father. This prayer acknowledges our dependence on God's mercy and love. It expresses our hope in all that God has promised.

"Deliver us, Lord, from every evil,
and grant us peace in our day.
In your mercy keep us free from sin
and protect us from all anxiety
as we wait in joyful hope
for the coming of our Savior, Jesus Christ."

Jesus promises us: "I will see you again, and your hearts will rejoice, and no one will take your joy away from you . . . . I say to you, whatever you ask the Father in my name he will give you. Ask and you will receive, so that your joy may be complete" (John 16:22–24).

In Jesus' name, we can ask God to continue to work through each one of us so that we may one day experience that complete and perfect kingdom he has prepared for us.

2.

VOCABULARY

hope: the belief and trust in all that God has promised through Jesus and the Church

Beatitudes: the basic principles of life in God's kingdom

heaven: unending happiness with God and with all who love God and one another

hell: everlasting separation from God and all those who love God

communion of saints: the entire community of God's people, whether living or dead

---

THIS IS OUR FAITH HERITAGE

The Beatitudes are the basic principles of life in God's kingdom. When we live the Beatitudes, we work for the fulfillment of God's kingdom of peace, love, and justice. We have trust in God's promise of eternal life to those who faithfully follow Jesus.

Kingdom People

Dorothy Day and Peter Maurin

Dorothy Day and Peter Maurin (MAWR ihn) founded the Catholic Worker movement in the United States. Together they started a newspaper (1933 – present) devoted to justice and equality. They opened shelters for the poor and soup kitchens to feed the hungry. They lived simply and encouraged others to do the same. Dorothy said that if someone had two coats, their second coat belonged to the poor. She said this was the responsibility of every Christian. Dorothy and Peter were poor in spirit.

Mother Teresa

Mother Teresa has been called a "Living example of the Beatitudes." She went from her convent many years ago to serve the poor, sick, and dying people of Calcutta, India. Today she and her sisters try to see Christ in the poor people to whom they minister. Mother Teresa has won many awards for her work with the neglected people of the world, but she accepts these awards only to help people understand the injustices that exist in our world.

Trevor Farrell

When Trevor Farrell was only twelve years old, a newscast inspired him to reach out to others. On a cold winter evening in their suburban Philadelphia home, the Farrells saw a television news segment about street people. Later that night, the family drove into the city.

Trevor gave a homeless man sleeping on a steam grate a pillow and blanket. As the man took the blanket, he said, "God bless you." Trevor began to post notices about the needs of the street people. He urged his classmates, members of the Church, neighbors, and people who came into his father's shop to contribute warm clothes and food. Many people have joined Trevor in caring for the poor. They generously donate their time to make soup and sandwiches to distribute. They collect medicine and clothing to take to the homeless. Trevor reminds us that we can look for ways to serve our neighbors right in our own hometown.

Martin Luther King, Jr.

Dr. Martin Luther King, Jr. had a dream. Martin's dream was that one day our children and all others would be judged on the content of their character rather than by the color of their skin. He led boycotts and peaceful demonstrations to put an end to racial discrimination against minorities. Many people did not want to hear Martin's message of equality and justice. He was beaten and unjustly imprisoned; his home was bombed. These persecutions did not prevent Martin from doing what God had called him to do. He even gave his life (April 4, 1968). The kingdom of God is his.

THE FRUITS OF THE HOLY SPIRIT.

When the gifts of the Holy Spirit are present within us, we see their effect in special qualities and attitudes that develop as we grow as disciples of Jesus, working to become a sign of God's kingdom in the world. These qualities are called the fruits of the Holy Spirit.

We recognize the signs of the presence of the Holy Spirit when we see charity, joy, peace, patience, kindness, goodness, endurance, humility, fidelity, and self-control evident in a person.

ACTIVITY

Choose one of the fruits of the Holy Spirit that you feel is developing in you. Write one effect you see in your behavior or in your attitude as a result of this fruit.

Answers will vary.

Kingdom Living Look back at the Beatitude chart. Think of one person you know or are aware of who is an example of living the Beatitudes. Tell what evidence you noticed that he or she has worked to bring God's kingdom of peace, love, and justice to the world. Tell about this person on the lines below.

Answers will vary. Possible answers might include ways

they have experienced mercy from a teacher or parent;

people they know who depend on God for what they need;

peace makers; and so on.

A Cinquain A cinquain (SIHNG kain) is a poem with five lines and eleven words. An example of a cinquain poem is at the left. An explanation for each line is on the right.

Beatitudes	One-word title
Happy living	Two words that explain the title
Comforting, sharing, working	Three action words about the title
Bringing peace, love, justice	Four words that express feelings about the title
Kingdom	One word referring to the title

Write your cinquain about one of the new ideas you learned about in this chapter, *The Kingdom of God* in these spaces.

Answers will vary.

Prayer of St. Francis

St. Francis of Assisi wrote this prayer. It reminds us to live in the spirit of the Beatitudes.

Lord, make me an instrument of your peace.
Where there is hatred, let me sow love;
    where there is injury, pardon;
    where their is doubt, faith;
    where there is despair, hope;
    where there is darkness, light;
    and where there is sadness, joy.
O Divine Master, grant that I may not seek
so much to be consoled as to console;
to be understood as to understand;
to be loved as to love.
For it is in giving that we receive;
    it is in pardoning that we are pardoned;
    and it is in dying
that we are born to eternal life.

Amen.

ACTIVITY   **Understanding Our Faith**

The Epistle of Saint _____

Imagine that you have been asked, as a member of the communion of saints, to write an epistle, or letter, to encourage other Catholic Christians to continue growing in holiness. Share with them your feelings about God's promises to you and how you feel drawn to respond to God's promises in your daily life.

Dear _____ ,

Answers will vary. Possible answers might include: God's

promise of an everlasting life of happiness for those who

put God first in their life. Encourage others to be willing

to speak the truth about God's will regardless of the

consequences.

_____

_____

A fellow Christian,

_____

1. When is Baptism usually celebrated?
2. Why is it the role of the community?
3. How does the celebration help the community to grow in faith?

Amen

Baptism

The Church welcomes new members in the sacrament of Baptism. Because Baptism unites us (1.) with Jesus in his death and resurrection, Baptism is usually celebrated on Sunday, when the Church community gathers together to remember Jesus' resurrection.

(2.) When Baptism is celebrated during a Mass, the parish community can join with the family and friends of the person who is being baptized. They pledge their love and support to help the new (3.) member grow in holiness. They are reminded of their responsibilities to live as baptized followers of Jesus.

WELCOMING

The presider of Baptism is a priest or a deacon. In the first part of the baptismal ceremony, called the "Reception of the Child," the priest greets the parents and godparents. This is often done at the entrance to the church. He reminds them of the joy they felt on the day of their child's birth and tells them that their child will be given new life

in Baptism. The family then joins the presider, lector, altar servers, and the ministers of Communion in processing to the altar.

When the processional song is finished, the parents, godparents, and the child who is being baptized stand with the priest near the altar. He asks the parents what name they have given their child and what they ask of God's Church. The parents call their child by name and ask that he or she be baptized. They may also respond by saying they want their child to be given the grace of Christ or faith.

4. Why is the marking with the sign of the cross a good indicator that the new member now belongs to Christ? (Answers will vary. They might include: The cross is a sign of Jesus' great love; as members of the Church

we will love others through service and sacrifice.

5. What prayer does the priest say at the anointing of the catechumen?

4. child by name and says, "The Christian community welcomes you with great joy. In its name I claim you for Christ our Savior by the sign of his cross. I now trace the cross on your forehead, and invite your parents (and godparents) to do the same."

THE LITURGY OF THE WORD

Then the Liturgy of the Word begins; everyone listens to God's word. During Sunday Mass, three readings are read: the first is from the Old Testament, the second reading is from the New Testament letters, and the last is the gospel.

The priest then gives a homily that explains the readings. His words help everyone understand the importance of Baptism and the responsibilities in living as baptized members of Christ's Church.

The intercessions, or Prayer of the Faithful, are said. We ask God to bless the child and to renew the new life of grace in all baptized persons. Then a litany is prayed which asks the saints' help and intercession.

ANOINTING BEFORE BAPTISM

The priest asks God to remove original sin from the child and make him or her a temple of God's glory. Then he anoints the child with the oil of catechumens:

5. "We anoint you with the oil of salvation in the name of Christ our Savior; may he strengthen you with his power, who lives and reigns for ever and ever."

The parents, godparents, and everyone present responds by saying, "Amen."

The priest explains the parent's and godparent's responsibilities in training their child in the faith. He asks them if they understand that they are called to bring up their child to "keep God's commandments as Christ taught us, by loving God and our neighbor."

After the parents and godparents have agreed to accept these responsibilities, the priest calls the

93

1. How do the parents and godparents express their faith in God and the Church?
2. What action does the priest do as part of the sign of Baptism?
3. What words does he use as part of the sign of Baptism?
4. What does the white garment signify?
5. What is the mission of parents and godparents?

BLESSING OF THE WATER

The priest blesses the water as he prays:

"We ask you, Father, with your Son
to send the Holy Spirit upon the water of this font.
May all who are buried with Christ in the death
of baptism
rise also with him to newness of life."

(1.) After the blessing of the water, the priest asks the parents and godparents to renew their baptismal vows. He leads them through a profession of their faith in God, Jesus, the Holy Spirit, and the Church. The priest says, "This is our faith. This is the faith of the Church. We are proud to profess it, in Christ Jesus our Lord."

THE BAPTISM

The priest then questions the parents and godparents. "Is it your will that N. should be baptized in the faith of the Church, which we have all professed with you?" They respond by saying, "It is."

(2.) The Baptism takes place as the priest calls the child by name and pours water on him or her three times, saying:

(3.) "N., I baptize you in the name of the Father, and of the Son, and of the Holy Spirit."

ANOINTING AFTER BAPTISM

The priest prays,
"The God of power and the Father of our Lord
Jesus Christ
has freed you from sin
and brought you to new life
through water and the Holy Spirit.

He now anoints you with the chrism of salvation, so that, united with his people,

you may remain forever a member of Christ who is Priest, Prophet, and King."

Everyone present responds by saying, "Amen." They watch in silence as the priest anoints the child's head with holy chrism, a holy oil.

THE WHITE GARMENT

Clothing the newly baptized with a white garment, the presider says, "N., you have become a new creation, and have clothed yourself in Christ." The white garment reminds us of our dignity as Christians.

(4.)

THE CANDLE

Standing near the lighted Easter candle, the priest invites the father or godfather to light a smaller candle from the flame. The priest says:

5. "Parents and godparents, this light is entrusted to you to be kept burning brightly. This child of yours has been enlightened by Christ. He (she) is to walk always as a child of the light. May he (she) keep the flame of faith alive in his (her) heart. When the Lord comes, may he (she) go out to meet him with all the saints in the heavenly kingdom."

With the lighted candle that the family will take home with them as a reminder of this

6. How does the community show that they welcome the new members of the Church?

important day, the family and presider process to the altar to pray. When the Baptism is celebrated during Mass, the Eucharistic celebration continues.

The celebration of Baptism ends with three blessings by the presider. He first blesses the mother and then the father. He prays that they are able to be the best teachers of their child by their example. He then blesses the entire community and prays that God will always make us faithful members of his holy people.

6. After the final blessing, the presider often formally introduces the new member to the parish community. We often show our feelings of joy and support by applauding. The baptism of new members is always a source of joy and renewal.

95

1. Who usually presides at the Confirmation Mass?
2. Who may be your sponsor?
3. Why is it good to ask your baptismal sponsor to be your Confirmation sponsor?

Confirmation

Confirmation is usually celebrated at a special

(1.) parish Mass at which the bishop or his representative presides. The Mass is attended by those who will receive Confirmation, their parents, and the Confirmation candidates' sponsors. Relatives, friends, and people who helped the candidates prepare for this special day might also be present.

(2.) The sponsor should be a person with deep Catholic faith who has celebrated all three Sacraments of Initiation. The sponsor's role is to present the candidate to the minister and to later help the candidate live out the baptismal promises that will be renewed during this ceremony.

(3.) Because of the close relationship between the sacraments of Baptism and Confirmation, it is desirable, if possible, that the baptismal sponsor also be the sponsor at Confirmation.

PRESENTATION OF THE CANDIDATES

The Sacrament of Confirmation is celebrated during the Liturgy of the Word. After the readings from Scripture, the pastor or another representative from the local parish, such as the Director of Religious Education, presents the candidates with their sponsors to the bishop. The presenter may tell the bishop how diligently the candidates prepared for the sacrament and express their eagerness to live the Christian life.

THE HOMILY OR INSTRUCTION

The bishop gives a homily or instruction to help everyone understand the mystery of

(4.) Confirmation. The Bishop may say: "The gift of the Holy Spirit which you are to receive will be a

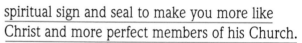

spiritual sign and seal to make you more like Christ and more perfect members of his Church.

. . . Be active members of the Church, alive in Jesus Christ. Under the guidance of the Holy Spirit give your lives completely in the service of all, as did Christ, who came not to be served but to serve."

RENEWAL OF BAPTISMAL PROMISES

After the homily the bishop questions the candidates. They make the the baptismal promises that their parents and godparents made for them on the day of their Baptism. You can find the renewal of the baptismal promises on page 59.

THE LAYING ON OF HANDS

The bishop asks the community to pray that God will send the Holy Spirit to strengthen the candidates. Then the bishop extends his hands over the candidates and sings or says:

"All-powerful God, Father of our Lord Jesus
    Christ,
by water and the Holy Spirit
you freed your sons and daughters from sin
and gave them new life.

96

4. What might the bishop say to us at Confirmation?
5. Name some of gifts the Holy Spirit will give us?
   (Look at the chart on page 34 to review the gifts.)
6. What is the sign of Confirmation?

Send your Holy Spirit upon them
to be their Helper and Guide.

5. Give them the spirit of <u>wisdom</u> and
   <u>understanding</u>,
the spirit of <u>right judgement</u> and <u>courage</u>,
the spirit of <u>knowledge</u> and <u>reverence</u>.
Fill them with the spirit of <u>wonder and awe</u> in
   your presence.
We ask this through Christ our Lord."
Everyone present says, "Amen."

THE ANOINTING WITH CHRISM

Each candidate stands before the bishop or priest
one at a time. The sponser places his right hand
on the candidate's shoulder and tells the bishop
the candidate's name.

6. <u>The bishop uses chrism to trace the sign of the
cross on the forehead of each person being
confirmed. As he does this, he calls them by name
and says, "N., be sealed with the Gift of the Holy
Spirit."</u> Each candidate responds by saying,
"Amen." Then the bishop says, "Peace be with
you," and the newly confirmed responds, "And
also with you." This is the sign of the sacrament
of Confirmation.

THE GENERAL INTERCESSIONS

Prayers are said for the newly confirmed, their
parents, godparents, and sponsers, the Church,
and for people of every race and nation that the
Spirit's work may "continue to grow in the hearts
of all who believe."

During the Preparation of the Gifts, some of the
newly confimed may bring the gifts of bread and
wine to the altar. The Mass continues, with the
bishop presiding. During the Communion Rite,
the newly confirmed and all present may be
invited to receive the full sign of the Eucharist by
sharing both the Eucharistic bread and wine.
Those candidates of catechetical age who have
not done so receive the Eucharist to complete
their Christian initiation.

At the end of the Mass, the bishop prays a final
blessing.

"God our Father,
complete the work you have begun
and keep the gifts of your Holy Spirit
active in the hearts of your people.
Make them ready to live his Gospel
and eager to do his will.
May they never be ashamed
to proclaim to all the world Christ crucified
living and reigning for ever and ever.
Amen.

And may the blessing of almighty God
the Father, and the Son, and the Holy Spirit
come upon you and remain with you
      for ever."
Everyone responds, "Amen."

The Confirmation liturgy ends with a
recessional song. The Holy Spirit will continue to
work through the lives of the newly confirmed,
helping them to live as witnesses to Christ.

The Mass

On Sundays, or Saturday evenings, the Catholic Christian community gathers to celebrate the Eucharist. This celebration is called the Eucharistic liturgy, or the Mass.

(1.) The celebration of the Mass is our greatest act of worship. During the Mass we praise and thank God for all his gifts, especially the gift of his Son, Jesus. We remember Jesus' sacrificial death on the cross and his resurrection from the dead. We are united with Jesus and the Church community as we share a special meal in his memory.

INTRODUCTORY RITES

The Mass begins with the Introductory Rites that help us to participate more fully in the liturgy. (2.) These prayers and actions prepare our minds and hearts to celebrate the Mass.

During the Entrance Song or Prayer, the priest and other ministers process to the altar. The reader carries the Lectionary, the book of readings from the Bible that are proclaimed at Mass. If a deacon is assisting the priest who is presiding, he will join the procession, along with the servers, and the ministers of Communion.

When the priest reaches the altar, he invites us to make the Sign of the Cross with him. Then he greets the community by saying, "The grace of our Lord Jesus Christ and the love of God and the fellowship of the Holy Spirit be with you all." And we reply, "And also with you."

During the Penitential Rite, we ask God and the Church community for forgiveness. One of the ways we sometimes do this is to pray the following prayer together:

"I confess to almighty God,
and to you, my brothers and sisters,
that I have sinned through my own fault
in my thoughts and in my words,
in what I have done,
and in what I have failed to do;
and I ask blessed Mary, ever virgin,
all the angels and saints,
and you, my brothers and sisters,
to pray for me to the Lord our God."

In another form of the Penitential Rite, the priest asks us to think about our lives and then prays three short prayers.

Priest: Lord Jesus, you raised us to new life: Lord, have mercy.
People: Lord, have mercy.
Priest: Lord Jesus, you forgive us our sins: Christ, have mercy.
People: Christ, have mercy.
Priest: Lord Jesus, you feed us with your body and blood: Lord, have mercy.
People: Lord, have mercy.

The priest then says: "May almighty God have mercy on us, forgive our sins, and bring us to everlasting life." We answer, "Amen."

(3.) We next <u>praise and honor God</u> by reciting or singing the Gloria.

"Glory to God in the highest,
    and peace to his people on earth.

Lord God, heavenly King,
almighty God and Father,
    we worship you, we give you thanks,
    we praise you for your glory.

Lord Jesus Christ, only Son of the Father,
Lord God, Lamb of God,
you take away the sin of the world:
    have mercy on us;
you are seated at the right hand of the Father:
    receive our prayer.

For you alone are the Holy One,
you alone are the Lord,
you alone are the Most High,
    Jesus Christ,
    with the Holy Spirit,
    in the glory of God the Father. Amen.

The Introductory Rite concludes with the Opening Prayer. The priest invites us to pray briefly in silence. Then he extends his hands and offers a prayer which reflects the theme of the Mass or the Church season.

1. From where is the first reading taken?
2. From what part of the Bible is the second reading on Sunday taken?
3. How do we show respect for the good news?
4. What does the priest or deacon say to announce the end of the gospel?
5. How do we respond to the gospel reading?
6. How would you describe the eucharistic prayer?

THE LITURGY OF THE WORD

The first major part of the Mass is the Liturgy of the Word. In the Liturgy of the Word, we listen and respond to God's Word. On Sundays we listen to three readings.

(1.) The first reading is from the Old Testament. The Responsorial Psalm follows the first reading. As we pray this psalm, we can ask God for mercy and forgiveness or give praise and thanks to God. We respond by repeating or singing the refrain.

(2.) The second reading is from the New Testament. It is usually taken from the epistles, or letters, of Jesus' disciples to the first Christian communities. This reading gives us advice in living the Christian life. The first and second readings may be read by a man or woman who ministers to the community by procaiming God's word. After each reading the reader says, "This is the Word of the Lord." We respond by saying, "Thanks be to God."

We stand for the alleluia or gospel acclamation. The word *alleluia* means "to give praise to God." We praise God for his living Word, Jesus, who (3.) speaks to us in the gospel. We remain standing throughout the reading of the gospel as a sign of respect and love for the good news of Jesus' life, death, and resurrection.

The gospel is read by the priest or the deacon who is assisting him. The priest prepares to read by praying silently. If the deacon is to read the gospel, he will ask the presider for his blessing. The priest will say, "The Lord be in your heart and on your lips that you may worthily proclaim his gospel."

After reading the gospel, the priest or deacon (4.) says, "This is the gospel of the Lord." We respond (5.) by saying, "Praise to you, Lord Jesus Christ."

A homily follows the reading of the gospel. As we have learned, the priest or deacon explains the readings in the homily. He tells us how we can be a better sign of God's kingdom by following God's word.

We stand to make the Profession of Faith. We express our belief in God, Jesus, the Holy Spirit, and the Church by praying one of the ancient creeds of the Church. We can pray the Apostles' Creed or the Nicene Creed on page 116.

The Liturgy of the Word ends with the community praying the general intercessions, or prayers of the faithful. We pray for our needs, and the needs of the Church and the world. We also pray for Church leaders, the sick, and those who have died. We may respond to each of the intercessions by praying, "Lord, hear our prayer," or another appropriate response.

LITURGY OF THE EUCHARIST

The second major part of the Mass is the Liturgy of the Eucharist. During this part of the (6.) celebration, we unite ourselves with Jesus in a prayer of praise and thanksgiving.

The Liturgy of the Eucharist begins with the preparation of the gifts and altar. Bringing gifts of bread and wine to the altar, we offer these gifts

7. What do we offer at the preparation of the gifts?
8. When does the bread and wine become the body and blood of Jesus?
9. What words of the Last Supper are used to consecrate the bread and wine?

7. to God in memory of Jesus, who gave his life for us. We also offer ourselves to God and ask God to unite us with Jesus and to work through us to build up the Body of Christ.

The bread and wine are placed on the altar. Saying the Prayer over the Gifts, the priest asks God to bless the bread and wine which will become our spiritual food and drink. He prays that God will accept our offerings. We respond by saying,

"May the Lord accept the sacrifice at your hands
for the praise and glory of his name,
for our good, and the good of all his Church."

8. The eucharistic prayer then begins. During this part of the Mass the bread and wine will become the body and blood of Jesus. The eucharistic prayer begins with the preface. In the preface we praise God's presence in our lives and thank God for the gift of salvation. We lift our minds and hearts to God as we pray or sing:

"Holy, holy, holy Lord, God of power and might.
Heaven and earth are full of your glory.
Hosanna in the highest.
Blessed is he who comes in the name of the Lord.
Hosanna in the highest."

We kneel as the priest continues the eucharistic prayer. One of them follows:

"Father, you are holy indeed,
and all creation rightly gives you praise.
All life, all holiness comes from you
through your Son, Jesus Christ our Lord,
by the working of the Holy Spirit.
From age to age you gather a people to yourself,
so that from east to west
a perfect offering may be made
to the glory of your name.

And so, Father, we bring you these gifts.
We ask you to make them holy by the power of
    your Spirit,
that they may become the body and blood
of your Son, our Lord Jesus Christ,
at whose command we celebrate this eucharist.

9. On the night he was betrayed,
he took bread and gave you thanks and praise.
He broke the bread, gave it to his disciples,
    and said:
Take this, all of you, and eat it:
this is my body which will be given up for you.

When supper was ended, he took the cup.
Again he gave you thanks and praise,
gave the cup to his disciples, and said:
Take this, all of you, and drink from it:
this is the cup of my blood,
the blood of the new and everlasting covenant.
It will be shed for you and for all
so that sins may be forgiven.
Do this in memory of me."

The priest elevates the body and blood of Christ and we proclaim our belief in the mystery of Jesus' life, death, resurrection, and presence with us now. We pray, "Christ has died, Christ is risen, Christ will come again," or a similar response.

The priest then prays on behalf of us, the family of God. He prays for our unity and that we may become one body through Jesus. He also prays that God will welcome those who have died into his kingdom. The priest then holds up the chalice and Eucharistic bread. He prays:

(1.) "Through him,
with him,
in him,
in the unity of the Holy Spirit,
all glory and honor is yours,
almighty Father,
for ever and ever."

We respond by singing or reciting the Great Amen. We express our belief in all that has happened during the eucharistic prayer when we respond "Amen."

102

2. How do we exchange the sign of peace?
3. What prayer does the priest pray as he holds up the consecrated bread before distributing communion?

4. What does the priest or eucharistic minister say as we receive communion? Our reply?
5. What two options do we have for receiving the Eucharistic bread?

THE COMMUNION RITE

Before we share the body and blood of Christ, we pray the Our Father together. Then the priest prays for peace and unity. He says, "The peace of the Lord be with you always." We respond,
(2.) "And also with you." We exchange a sign of peace, by shaking hands, hugging, or kissing the people around us. This is a sign of the unity and love of the Christian community.

As the priest breaks the Eucharistic bread, which makes us one in the Body of Christ, we ask Jesus for mercy and peace.

"Lamb of God, you take away the sins of the world:
    have mercy on us.
Lamb of God, you take away the sins of the world:
    have mercy on us.
Lamb of God, you take away the sins of the world:
    grant us peace."

During Jesus' time, it was customary to sacrifice and eat a roasted lamb at the Passover meal. This reminded the Jewish people of God's love for them and how he freed them from slavery in Egypt. We call Jesus the Lamb of God because he sacrificed himself to save us from sin and death.

The priest elevates the Eucharistic bread and says,

(3.) "This is the Lamb of God
    who takes away the sins of the world.
Happy are those who are called to his supper."

We believe in Jesus' power to strengthen us to follow him.
We pray, "Lord, I am not worthy to receive you, but only say the word and I shall be healed."

We can now receive Jesus in Holy Communion. The priest or eucharistic minister says, "The body
(4.) of Christ." We answer "Amen" to express our faith in the real presence of Jesus in the bread and
(5.) wine. We can receive the Eucharistic Bread in our hands or on our tongues.

After Communion, we can silently offer a prayer of thanksgiving to God. We can ask God to help us live as a follower of Jesus and a baptized member of his Church. We also join the community in singing a Communion song.

CONCLUDING RITE

In the Concluding Rite, the priest blesses us and sends us forth. He says, "Go in peace to love and serve the Lord." We respond "Thanks be to God." We are grateful that we are able to share in Jesus' mission of bringing the kingdom to the world. We do this by loving and serving others, as Jesus did.

1. Why do we celebrate Reconciliation?
2. On what moral standards is the examination of conscience found on these pages based?

3. Why does the priest greet us in both Jesus' name and that of the community? (Because we have sinned against both and will be reunited to both.)

Reconciliation

AN EXAMINATION OF CONSCIENCE

We have learned that the sacrament of Reconciliation is one of the sacraments of healing. In the sacrament of Reconciliation, we celebrate God's mercy and forgiveness. We are reunited with God and the Church community through this sacrament.

Before we celebrate the sacrament of Reconciliation it is important that we identify the attitudes and actions which are preventing us from being a sign of God's kingdom. We do this by praying to the Holy Spirit for guidance and examining our consciences. An examination of conscience helps us to grow in holiness and recognize our sins. On page 66, we learned one way to examine our conscience. We also examine our conscience at Mass during the Penitential Rite when we think of our sins and ask God and Jesus to have mercy on us.

During an examination of conscience, we ask ourselves how we are living as members of the Body of Christ. We might review the Ten Commandments, Jesus' teachings on the Great Commandment, the New Commandment of Jesus, or the Beatitudes. The examination of conscience below is based on the Beatitudes that are found on page 86.

- Do I recognize how much I need God? Do I show my love for God?

- Do I show care and concern for others?

- Do I share my gifts and talents with others?

- Am I a sign of God's peace, love, and justice for others? Do I treat others fairly? Do I share my possessions with others?

- Am I forgiving? Do I treat others with compassion?

- Do I try to know God's will for me?

- Am I a peacemaker? Do I pray for peace? Do I try to settle disagreements and arguments?

- Do I stand up for my beliefs? Do I make good moral decisions even when it is not easy? Do I respect the rights of others?

CELEBRATING RECONCILIATION

After we examine our conscience, we may recognize that we have sinned by failing to live as a follower of Jesus. When we are sorry for our sins, we can receive God's forgiveness through the sacrament of Reconciliation.

This sacrament can be celebrated communally with a group, but even then we tell our sins privately to the priest. Parishes often celebrate the sacrament communally during Advent or Lent.

We can also celebrate the sacrament of Reconciliation alone with a priest. Individual Reconciliation can be celebrated any time we feel the need for God's mercy and forgiveness. There are six steps in receiving the Rite of Reconciliation of Individual Penitents. The word *pentitent* refers to someone who is sorry for his or her sins and is seeking God's forgiveness.

1. *We prepare ourselves to celebrate Reconciliation by prayer.* We ask the Holy Spirit to give us the wisdom to recognize and be sorry for our sins. We review our examination of conscience.

2. *We are welcomed in Jesus' name.* We enter the reconciliation room or confessional. We can choose to speak to the priest directly,

104

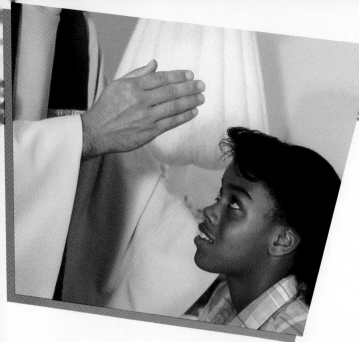

4. How does the penance help us to be better?
5. What does the word *absolution* mean? (forgive)
6. Why is Penance often called "the sacrament of peace?"

3. face to face or behind the screen. Either way the priest greets us in the name of Jesus and the Church community. We make the sign of the cross together. He asks us to have confidence in God's mercy and love. He says,

"May God, who has enlightened every heart, help you to know your sins
and trust in his mercy."

3. *We listen to the word of God.* A story from Scripture is read aloud. This can be read by the priest or the penitent. The reading of God's word reminds us of our need for forgiveness and trust in God's mercy.

4. *We confess our sins and accept our penance.* We tell our sins to the priest who represents God and the Christian community. The priest may ask questions to help us make a complete confession. He helps us express sorrow for our sins. He talks with us about how we can better live a moral life.

Then the priest gives us a penance to do to make up for our sins and show that we want to live a new life. The penance may be prayer or an act of service to our neighbor or someone we have hurt. Our penance helps us to be healed of our sinful condition. It helps restore our relationship with God and our neighbors.

5. *We pray a prayer of sorrow.* We can pray the Act of Contrition on page 115, or another prayer of sorrow. We can pray:

Lord Jesus, Son of God
have mercy on me, a sinner.

6. *We receive absolution (forgiveness).* The priest extends his arms over us and says:

"God, the Father of mercies,
through the death and resurrection of
   his Son
has reconciled the world to himself
and sent the Holy Spirit among us
for the forgiveness of sins;
through the ministry of the Church
may God give you pardon and peace,
and I absolve you from your sins
in the name of the Father, and of the Son,
and of the Holy Spirit."
We respond, "Amen."

The priest dismisses us with a brief prayer. He may say, "The Lord has freed you from your sins. Go in peace," or "The Lord has freed you from sin. May he bring you safely to his kingdom in heaven."

After the celebration of the sacrament of Reconciliation we can pray privately, thanking God for the gifts of mercy and forgiveness. Our prayer can express our desire to avoid sin in the future and to live always as a follower of Jesus. We remember to do the penance the priest has given us.

The sacrament of Reconciliation is often called the sacrament of peace because we are freed from our sins and receive God's peace. We thank God for this gift by sharing God's peace and forgiveness with others.

1. What does the word *Advent* mean?
2. What is the first coming of Jesus that we celebrate during Advent?
3. What is the second coming of Christ?
4. What will happen at the third coming?
5. What does the name Immanuel mean?
6. Look at Isaiah's poem. What are some other names we call God?

Advent — Christmas

Advent is one of the major seasons of the Church year. *Advent* means "coming." It is a time to reflect on Jesus coming into our world and his promise to be with us always. During Advent, we celebrate the three comings of Jesus.

The first coming of Jesus is his birth in Bethlehem 2000 years ago. Advent is the time of preparation for Christmas as we think about the meaning of the Incarnation in our lives. Actually, the Church began to prepare for Christmas only after the fourth century, when the celebration of Jesus' birth on December 25 was first established. (This date was chosen to take the place of the pagan celebration in honor of the sun.) By the sixth century, the Church had set aside a fixed time to prepare for the celebration of Jesus' coming at Christmas.

The second coming is the coming of the kingdom of God that is happening now in our everyday world. Because Jesus kept his promise and is always with us, we can celebrate his presence among us now and reflect upon our mission to work with him as he brings about God's kingdom of peace, love, and justice.

The third coming that we reflect upon during Advent is the coming of Jesus at the end of time when God's kingdom of perfect peace, love, and joy will reign in the world. Because we believe that Jesus will come in glory and that the kingdom will be fulfilled at that time, we have great hope.

The prohet Isaiah is frequently read during Advent because he spoke of a savior whom Christians know as Jesus: "A virgin shall be with child, and bear a son, and shall call him Immanuel." *Immanuel* means "God–is–with–us."

"The people who walked in darkness have seen a great light;

Upon those who dwelt in the land of gloom a light has shone.

For a child is born to us, a son is given us; upon his shoulder dominion rests.

They name him Wonder-Counselor, God-Hero, Father-Forever, Prince of Peace.

His dominion is vast and forever peaceful,

From David's throne, and over his kingdom, which he confirms and sustains

By judgment and justice, both now and forever."

Isaiah 9:1, 5–6

We prepare for the coming of Immanuel, Jesus, who will work through our lives to help us be a better sign of his presence. We make ourselves ready to celebrate Jesus' rebirth in our lives and hearts by living the Beatitudes, the New Commandment of Love, obeying the Ten Commandments, and doing works of mercy.

Christmas celebrates Jesus' Incarnation. To celebrate fully, the Church sets aside not only a day but a whole liturgical season. We reflect and joyfully remember that Jesus is God becoming human. During this season, several important feasts reveal "God–is–with–us." Beginning with Christmas, the celebration of Jesus' birth, we continue on to the feast of Cana. You remember that it was at Cana that Jesus performed his first miracle when he changed water into wine. This is the first time that people saw God present in him. The feast of the Epiphany shows us that God made Jesus known to all people as the Magi honored him. Finally the feast of the Baptism of the Lord, when we remember that God the Father called Jesus "My beloved Son," is celebrated.

By participating in each feast, our faith grows and we can ask God to help us share it with others.

7. Why do you think we call Jesus the "Prince of Peace?"
8. What does it mean to celebrate "God is with us" at Christmas? at Epiphany? when we read the story of the wedding of Cana? at the Baptism of the Lord? (Answers will vary, but might include how we know of God's presence at each of these events. (Read Luke 2:1–20; Matthew 2:1–12, 3:1–17; John 2:1–12.)

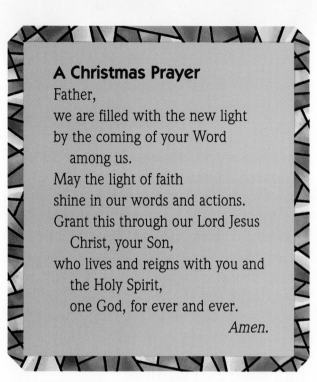

A Christmas Prayer

Father,
we are filled with the new light
by the coming of your Word
    among us.
May the light of faith
shine in our words and actions.
Grant this through our Lord Jesus
    Christ, your Son,
who lives and reigns with you and
    the Holy Spirit,
    one God, for ever and ever.
                    Amen.

ACTIVITY

The Advent Wreath

The Advent wreath is a traditional Advent symbol. The evergreen branches are a sign of everlasting life. The shape of the wreath reminds us that God is unending and that our lives with God will never end if we live as disciples of Jesus. The candles represent Jesus, the light of the world. There is one candle for each of the four weeks of Advent.

During the first week of Advent we light one candle on the wreath. We pray that our lives will reflect the light of Christ. We add another candle each week, as a sign that Jesus' presence in our lives is increasing through our prayers and loving service to others.

1. What is Lent?
2. How did the early Christians observe Lent?
3. What changed the way Lent was celebrated?

4. What two aspects of Lent does the Church emphasize today?

Lent — Easter

Easter, the greatest feast of the Church year, celebrates Jesus' resurrection. We remember that when God raised Jesus from the dead, Jesus **(1.)** shared the hope of everlasting life with us. Lent is the liturgical season when we ask that our lives be transformed so that we can better share in Jesus' new life.

(2.) In the early Church, Lent was observed as a time of intense preparation for the sacrament of Baptism that would take place at Easter. The catechumens, who were mainly adults, prepared to celebrate the three sacraments of initiation. They prayed, fasted, and did penance to purify themselves to become full members of the Church, the Body of Christ. The already initiated members of the Church community recalled their own baptisms and reflected on how they could better follow Jesus.

(3.) In time infant baptism became more common and the process of renewal through the initiation of new adult members was lost. Lent became a time of repentance, when the Church community focused on turning away from sin and returning to God with a new heart.

In today's Church, both of these important **(4.)** aspects of Lent are emphasized. Lent is seen as a time of conversion or *metanoia,* which means "change of heart." Through the *Rite of Christian Initiation of Adults,* we journey with the catechumens as they prepare to celebrate the sacraments of initiation at the Easter Vigil. Their rebirth as children of God through the waters of Baptism is an opportunity for all members of the community to renew their baptismal commitment. Their confirmation reminds us that we have sealed our covenant to witness to our world. Their celebration of the Eucharist enlivens our faith in the real presence of Jesus under the appearance of bread and wine.

Lent is also a time of repentance, when we examine our lives to become aware of what is preventing us from living out our baptismal **(5.)** commitment. We can set aside time to pray and reflect. We can celebrate the sacrament of Reconcilation as a sign of our willingness to change our hearts. We can participate in parish Lenten programs and activities.

THE EASTER TRIDUUM

Observing Lent fully helps us to enter into the **(6.)** solemn celebration of Easter. Because Easter is the highpoint of the liturgical year, we celebrate it for **(7.)** three days called the Easter triduum. The Church community commemorates the Lord's Supper on **(8.)** Holy Thursday evening. On the next day, Good Friday, the community gathers to reflect on what Jesus' death means to all people.

Then on Holy Saturday night, the community assembles in a darkened church to celebrate the **(9.)** resurrection with signs and symbols. The Easter candle is lit and lifted up high while the deacon or priest sings, "Christ our light." We continue to celebrate the resurrection with the signs of Baptism and the breaking of the bread and the sharing of the wine in the Eucharist.

On Easter Sunday, the Church community hears the Easter message proclaimed. God has raised Jesus Christ from the dead. Alleluia!

The celebration continues for forty days called Eastertime.

5. What can we do to show we have changed our hearts?
6. What is the triduum?
7. What do we celebrate on Holy Thursday?

8. What does Good Friday commemorate?
9. In what ways do we celebrate Jesus' resurrection at the Easter vigil?

A Sign of the Cross Ritual

This ritual will help you to recall that Jesus asks us to use our whole being to build up the Church. Find a partner and face one another. Your teacher will read the directions in the parentheses aloud, then the words of the ritual. Repeat them as you do the action described.

(Make the sign of the cross on your partner's ears.)
I sign your ears with the sign of the cross:
may you hear the words of Christ.

(Make the sign of the cross over your partner's heart.)
I sign you with the sign of the cross:
may you welcome Christ into your heart by faith.

(Make the sign of the cross on your partner's shoulders.)
I sign your shoulders with the sign of the cross:
may you have the strength of Christ.

All: May you live with Jesus now and forever. In the name of the Father, and of the Son, and of the Holy Spirit, Amen.

Adapted from the
Rite of Christian Initiation for Adults

ACTIVITY

AN EASTER BIBLE HUNT

Use your Bible to find the Scripture quotations below. Match each quotation with the liturgy described below.

A. __1__ Luke 24:1–12

B. __3__ Luke 22:14–20

C. __2__ Matthew 26:36 – 27:54

1. On Easter Sunday the community hears the Easter message proclaimed. God has raised Jesus Christ from the dead.

2. On Good Friday, we journey with Jesus to Calvary. We thank Jesus for his sacrifice on the cross.

3. On Holy Thursday, we reflect on the Last Supper. We celebrate the institution of the Eucharist in memory of Jesus.

Glossary / Index

Christ
A Greek word meaning "God's anointed one" *22*

Christian
A baptized follower of Jesus *30*

Communion of saints
The entire community of God's people, whether living or dead *87*

Confirmation
The second sacrament of initiation which strengthens the new life we received at Baptism *54, 96–97*

Conscience
The ability to judge whether something is right or wrong *31*

Contrition
Sorrow for sin *67, 104–105*

Corporal Works of Mercy
Ways in which we serve the physical needs of others in Jesus' name *72*

Covenant
The relationship God established with Abraham, Moses, and the people of Israel; that Jesus established with the Church *7, 15, 16,*

Creation *13*

D

Deacon
An ordained minister who serves the poor and needy, spreads God's word by proclaiming the gospel, celebrates the sacraments by baptizing, presiding at weddings and burial services *71, 92, 98*

Devil *32*

Diocese
A group of parishes led by a bishop *48*

Dorothy Day *89*

E

Elizabeth, (cousin of Mary) *17*

Elizabeth Seton, Saint *57*

Eucharist
The sacrament that celebrates the presence of Jesus under the appearance of bread and wine, in the word of God, and in the gathered community *55, 56*

F

Faith
Belief and trust in God and in all that God has revealed *14*

Fortitude
The virtue of having the courage to resist temptation and choose the right action *81*

Francis de Sales, Saint *33*

Fruits of the Holy Spirit
Charity, joy, peace, patience, kindness, goodness, endurance, humility, fidelity, self–control *90*

G

Galilee *10, 13, 21*

Genesis
The first book of the Bible *13*

Prayers

Sign of the Cross

In the name of the Father,
and of the Son,
and of the Holy Spirit.

Amen.

Our Father

Our Father,
who art in heaven,
hallowed be thy name;
thy kingdom come;
thy will be done on earth
as it is in heaven.
Give us this day our daily bread;
and forgive us our trespasses
as we forgive those
who trespass against us;
and lead us not into temptation,
but deliver us from evil.

Amen.

Hail Mary

Hail Mary, full of grace!
The Lord is with you.
Blessed are you among women,
and blessed is the fruit of your womb, Jesus.
Holy Mary, Mother of God,
pray for us sinners
now and at the hour of our death.

Amen.

Communal Act of Repentance

I confess to almighty God,
and to you, my brothers and sisters,
that I have sinned through my own fault
in my thoughts and in my words,
in what I have done,
and in what I have failed to do;
and I ask blessed Mary, ever virgin,
all the angels and saints,
and you, my brothers and sisters,
to pray for me to the Lord our God.

An Act of Contrition

My God,
I am sorry for my sins with all my heart.
In choosing to do wrong
and failing to do good,
I have sinned against you
whom I should love above all things.
I firmly intend, with your help,
to do penance,
to sin no more,
and to avoid whatever leads me to sin.
Our Savior Jesus Christ
suffered and died for us.
In his name, my God, have mercy.

The Rite of Penance

115

Nicene Creed

We believe in one God,
    the Father, the Almighty,
    maker of heaven and earth,
    of all that is seen and unseen.

We believe in one Lord, Jesus Christ,
    the only Son of God,
    eternally begotten of the Father,
    God from God, Light from Light,
    true God from true God,
    begotten, not made,
    one in Being with the Father.
    Through him all things were made.
    For us men and for our salvation
        he came down from heaven:
by the power of the Holy Spirit
    he was born of the Virgin Mary,
        and became man.
For our sake he was crucified under
        Pontius Pilate,
    he suffered, died, and was buried.
    On the third day he rose again
        in fulfillment of the Scriptures;
    he ascended into heaven
        and is seated at the right hand of the Father.
He will come again in glory to judge the living
    and the dead,
and his kingdom will have no end.

We believe in the Holy Spirit, the Lord,
    the giver of life,
    who proceeds from the Father and the Son.
    With the Father and the Son he is worshiped
        and glorified.

He has spoken through the Prophets.
We believe in one holy catholic
    and apostolic Church.
We acknowledge one baptism
    for the forgiveness of sins.
We look for the resurrection of the dead,
    and the life of the world to come.
                                        Amen.

Apostles' Creed

I believe in God, the Father almighty,
    creator of heaven and earth.

I believe in Jesus Christ, his only Son, our Lord,
    He was conceived by the power
        of the Holy Spirit
        and born of the Virgin Mary.
    He suffered under Pontius Pilate,
        was crucified, died, and was buried.
    He descended to the dead.
    On the third day he rose again.
    He ascended into heaven,
        and is seated at the right hand of the Father.
    He will come again to judge the living
        and the dead.

I believe in the Holy Spirit,
    the holy catholic Church,
    the communion of saints,
    the forgiveness of sins,
    the resurrection of the body,
    and the life everlasting.
                                        Amen.

THIS IS OUR FAITH

IS OUR

FAITH

HERITAGE PROGRAM II
TEACHER EDITION

Author: **Kate Sweeney Ristow**

SILVER BURDETT & GINN
MORRISTOWN, N.J.

THIS IS OUR FAITH

Heritage Program, Book II

Consultants: Sister Mary Boys, Rev. Frank Sokol, Barbara Zanin

Readers: Deborah Hawks, Judith Conte

Nihil Obstat
Reverend Anselm Murray, O.S.B.
Censor Librorum

Imprimatur
✠ Most Reverend Frank J. Rodimer
Bishop of Paterson
March 6, 1989

©1990 Silver, Burdett & Ginn, Inc. All rights reserved. Printed in the United States of America.
ISBN 0-382-00730-1

CONTENTS

How to Use *This Is Our Faith Heritage II*

INTRODUCTION

Dear Catechist,

Welcome to *This Is Our Faith Heritage II*. You have accepted the special responsibility and challenge of introducing young people to the beliefs and traditions of the Catholic community. Some of the children with whom you will share faith may have been baptized as infants, while others are just preparing to become members of the Church. Then there may be those who have been trained in another Christian tradition.

What they all will have in common is that they will be unfamiliar with the teachings and practices of the Catholic Church.

Because of their different backgrounds, these junior-high-age youngsters may reflect a variety of attitudes. There will be the curious who will be inquisitive about the Christian message. Others may be initially unreceptive to the idea of learning about Jesus and his Church. In addition, there might be those who feel anxious about "being behind" their peers; there will always be those delightful children who are excited about the new identity and way of life to which you are introducing them.

THE PROGRAM

The purpose of *This Is Our Faith Heritage II* is to mainstream the junior-high youth with little or no previous religious education. Designed to be a tutorial program that can be completed within 13–20 lesson hours, depending upon the needs of the young person, the program may be used with one or more youngsters. More time will be needed if the young teens will receive one or several of the sacraments in conjunction with this program.

Recognizing the need for evangelization for these boys and girls, *This Is Our Faith Heritage II* begins with ten gospel stories so that the word of God may speak directly to them. These particular events in the life of Jesus have been chosen because they answer the question of why Jesus came and help describe Jesus' mission.

The stories may be read independently by the youngster who is already familiar with the Scriptures, or they may be read over the span of several sessions, taking into account the young person's reading ability and level of spiritual awareness. Special annotations appear in the Teacher's Edition of the pupil pages found in this guide. They are reading guide questions to help you discuss the gospel with the youngsters.

The second section of the program consists of ten one-hour catechetical lessons, including material on the sacraments, the Ten Commandments, the Beatitudes, and the New Commandment of Love. The following chart suggests how the lessons may be scheduled, depending upon the needs and ability of the youngsters since these chapters are content oriented.

The third part of the program, the "Amen" section, includes the rites of Baptism, Confirmation, Eucharist, and Reconciliation as well as material on Advent-Christmas and Lent-Easter. These chapters may be used to supplement the sacrament lessons or in conjunction with them, to review the rites the boys and girls may have previously celebrated, or to study the liturgy of the Church as a unit. Anyone who will be receiving any sacrament(s) as the culmination of this program will need to study the rite(s) in detail.

A special section of this guide called "For the Immediate Preparation of the Sacraments" may be used with these young people and their families. Special two-and-one-half hour to three-hour prayer sessions have been developed to help prepare the youngsters for the reception of the sacraments.

The blackline master booklet available with this program provides activity masters as well as parent letters and family prayer suggestions to provide interesting and meaningful opportunities for the young teens to think and respond creatively and to learn more about our Catholic faith and traditions.

Lesson Plans: Total Hours	13	15	16	18	20
Gospel Stories					
The Road to Emmaus		1 hr.	1 hr.	1 hr.	1 hr.
The Baptism of Jesus	1 hr.				1 hr.
Beginning His Ministry		1 hr.	1 hr.	1 hr.	1 hr.
The Ten Lepers				1 hr.	1 hr.
The Sinful Woman	1 hr.	1 hr.	1 hr.	1 hr.	1 hr.
The Feeding of the 5,000				1 hr.	1 hr.
The Passion, Part I		1 hr.	1 hr.	1 hr.	1 hr.
The Passion, Part II			1 hr.	1 hr.	1 hr.
The Resurrection	1 hr.	1 hr.	1 hr.	1 hr.	1 hr.
Mission of the Disciples					1 hr.
10 Doctrinal Lessons (chapters) Average time: 1 hr. each	10 hr.	10 hr.	10 hr.	10 hr.	10 hr.

OPTIONAL

Study of the Rites

Baptism (1 hr.)

Confirmation (1 hr.)

The Mass (1 hr.)

Reconciliation (1 hr.)

Study of the Rites is supplementary and must be added to the total hours, if you wish to use it. The content can be taught in one-hour segments.

Immediate Preparation for the Sacraments

Estimated Time: 2¹/₂–3 hrs.

Immediate Preparation for the Sacraments for those receiving one or more sacraments also may be added to the program.

LESSON PLANS

The Life of Jesus *from the Gospels*
The Ten Doctrinal Lessons
Family Sessions

The Appearance on the Road to Emmaus   *Luke 24:13–35*

OBJECTIVES

To help the young people
- learn the story of Emmaus
- meet the risen Jesus
- want to share the good news they learn about Jesus

SHARING THE STORY

In this gospel story the young people you are working with will meet the risen Jesus. They will learn how Jesus explained the Scriptures to his disciples and how they came to recognize him in the breaking of the bread. Your relationship to the youngsters models the disciples' experiences with Jesus on the road to Emmaus. In the coming weeks you will walk with these young teens, explaining our beliefs and helping them to recognize Jesus in the world, our Church, and the people they meet. As their faith develops, you can encourage them to share the good news with others, as Jesus' disciples did.

This section of *This Is Our Faith Heritage II* introduces the youngsters to Jesus through the gospels. The purpose is to open their minds and hearts to the word of God before beginning the more formal study of the doctrines and traditions of the Catholic Church presented in the next section of the book.

BEFORE READING THE STORY

Introduce yourself to the youngsters and tell them something about yourself. Invite each one to share something important about himself or herself. This might be a nickname, a hobby, a talent, or some interesting family background.

Present a *This Is Our Faith Heritage II* book to each young person. Briefly explain that in the first section they will meet Jesus and learn some of the stories about his life. Ask the young people to name some of the things they may already know about him. Make a list of the facts they name and have them decide what they think is the most important one. Tell them that they are going to read a gospel story in which two of Jesus' friends came to know something very important about Jesus. Let them discover the good news of his resurrection.

READING THE STORY

Use the annotated questions printed with the student text on pages iv–2 at the front of this book to promote discussion.

AFTER READING THE STORY

Use the Bible map located on the inside back cover of the student book to help the young people visualize the journey between Emmaus and Jerusalem. This will be very helpful, even though we do not know the exact locations of many of the ancient towns. Emmaus happens to be one of these. We do know that it was close to Jerusalem. Remind the youngsters that the disciples walked this distance in a hot, arid climate.

Discuss why the disciples returned to Jerusalem after they recognized Jesus. Ask the boys and girls what they do when they have good news, such as a great report card or an unexpected gift. Elicit from them that they probably share their good news with others. Emphasize that the disciples were eager to tell others that they had seen the risen Jesus.

Have the young people name the good news they learned about Jesus from this story. Help them focus on the reality of Jesus' resurrection and his willingness to help the disciples understand what had happened. Assure them that Jesus will help them as they explore his life and teachings.

USING BLACKLINE MASTERS

Use Activity Master 1 with this gospel story. Point out the family page. These are ways of helping the young people spread the good news at home.

The Preaching of John the Baptist *Matthew 3:1–2, 5–6, 11, 13–17*

OBJECTIVES

To help the young people
- learn the story of Jesus' baptism
- understand that Jesus is God's Son
- want to share in Jesus' loving relationship with God

SHARING THE STORY

In this session the youngsters will learn the story of Jesus' baptism. A detail that may need clarification is the river baptism. You can assure your group that baptism by immersion or dunking was a common practice during Jesus' time. Actually, it is a practice being restored in our own Church today. You may want to have the children find the Jordan River on the map.

The point you will want to make with the youngsters is the recognition of Jesus by John and, more importantly, by God his Father. John's mission was to prepare the world for Jesus. He did this by urging people to change the way they were living. When he met Jesus, he knew immediately that Jesus was the one he was preaching about. It is also clear that John did not want to baptize Jesus. The lesson here is that Jesus convinced John to baptize him because he wanted to fulfill God's plan for the world.

Help your group appreciate God's acknowledgment of Jesus as "my beloved Son." This story clearly states that the risen Jesus the disciples met on the road to Emmaus was the Son of God.

In later chapters of *This Is Our Faith Heritage II*, the youngsters will learn about the Blessed Trinity, the Holy Spirit, and Baptism. For now it is appropriate that they begin to recognize Jesus' unique relationship of "beloved Son" to the Father and his willingness to do God's will.

BEFORE READING THE STORY

Talk with the youngsters about times that they have been publicly acknowledged for an achievement. Discuss how they were recognized or praised and how they felt about their accomplishment. This will be a positive experience for the group if you encourage, rather than insist, that each youngster share a story about themselves.

Tell the young people that in today's story they will learn about a time Jesus was acknowledged by his Father.

READING THE STORY

Use the annotated questions printed with the student text on pages 2–3 to ensure that the youngsters understand the material being presented. You might ask the question first and have them find the answer.

AFTER READING THE STORY

Discuss the question of why John was reluctant to baptize Jesus. Help the young people appreciate that John recognized that Jesus was the one he had been preaching about. He knew that Jesus did not need to repent or change the way he was living. Explain that Jesus wanted to be baptized because he understood it as part of his Father's plan or will for him.

Emphasize that this story tells us that Jesus was God's "beloved Son" and that he had a great desire to fulfill his Father's plan for the world. Tell the youngsters that Jesus invites us to share in a special relationship with him, and through him with the Father. Help them to become aware that as they grow in faith, they will feel a close bond with God and Jesus.

USING BLACKLINE MASTERS

Use Activity Master 2 with this gospel story. Point out the family page for use at home.

The Beginning of the Galilean Ministry *Luke 4:14–21*

OBJECTIVES

To help the children
- learn that Jesus taught in God's name
- understand Jesus' mission
- grow in awareness that God sent Jesus to save the people

SHARING THE STORY

In this story, the youngsters will read about the beginning of Jesus' active ministry. They will begin to see God's plan for the salvation of the world unfold through Jesus.

Everything that Jesus did — teaching in God's name, healing, forgiving, and bringing the good news of God's love to the poor — was directed toward a clear purpose. Jesus was sent by God to save people. As Jesus read Isaiah's words, he claimed them as the description of his own mission. Christians see these words as a proclamation of Jesus that he was to bring God's kingdom of peace and love to the world.

After reading, Jesus sits down and begins to teach, showing that Isaiah's words describe God's plan for him. It would be surprising if the worshipers in the synagogue fully understood Jesus.

The Jews of this time were looking for a "messiah." They had many different ways of thinking about this special person that God promised to send to save them. Among these were: a royal ruler, a deliverer from Roman oppression, or a Spirit-filled person. Regardless of what kind of a messiah they expected, they all longed for someone who would usher in God's reign of peace and justice. Later some would come to understand that Jesus truly fit this role of the one who would establish God's reign in the world and they would apply the term "messiah" to him.

It is the same with the young people you are sharing your faith with. At this point it will be difficult for them to understand how Jesus frees and saves us. They need more time and information to develop their relationship with Jesus. Now, it is enough for them to know that God sent Jesus to bring peace and justice.

BEFORE READING THE STORY

Invite the youngsters to describe and discuss a favorite teacher. Allow sufficient time for them to share their stories.

Tell them that in this gospel story they will learn about God's plan for Jesus. They will begin to understand that Jesus came to show us how to live according to God's plan. This is why we call Jesus, "Teacher."

READING THE STORY

Use the annotated questions on pages 3–4 at the front of this book for discussion. Perhaps, you might want the youngsters to underscore the answers or highlight them with a marker to review the main ideas.

AFTER READING THE STORY

Explain to your group that the people who heard Jesus preach that day in the synagogue did not yet know the great things that he would do for them and all the people. Help them appreciate that we, too, have much to learn about Jesus in the coming weeks.

Talk with the young people about their experience of coming to know Jesus. Who first told them about him and what was their response?

Share your own experience of coming to know Jesus. Stories such as these help young people recognize that Jesus continues to announce himself to us, just as he did in the synagogue in Nazareth.

USING THE BLACKLINE MASTERS

Use Activity Master 3 with this story. Encourage the youngsters to do this activity at home to involve the family. Point out the family page to take home.

The Cleansing of Ten Lepers *Luke 17:11–19*

OBJECTIVES

To help the young people
- learn the story of Jesus curing ten lepers
- understand that Jesus heals and saves all people
- want to express gratitude to Jesus

SHARING THE STORY

In this gospel story the young people will continue to learn about Jesus' mission: he came to save and heal all people. Help the youngsters understand that the lepers Jesus healed were Samaritans. These people and the Jews had become enemies long ago and did not get along or even associate with each other. You will want to emphasize that Jesus' compassion is not limited to any one class or race. It extends even to those regarded as enemies. Jesus cares about all people and wants everyone to know that they are saved through him. In subsequent chapters you will share more with the youngsters about how Jesus saves people. Here, you have a tangible example of Jesus demonstrating his power to save by freeing people from a disfiguring disease.

The leper who returned to thank Jesus is an excellent example for the youngsters. You can help them appreciate that we should be thankful for the blessings we have received and for all the good things in life. Later in *This Is Our Faith Heritage II,* they will learn that God is the source of all good and that thankfulness is an appropriate attitude for all God's people to have.

BEFORE SHARING THE STORY

Invite the young people to name some things for which they are thankful. They might make their own list, jotting down who they want to thank, what the person did, and why they appreciate it. Discuss: Have they expressed their gratitude and appreciation? How can they do this?

Tell the youngsters that in today's gospel story they will read about a man who thanked Jesus for a gift he had been given. It is an example of how we should be thankful.

READING THE STORY

Pause to use the annotated questions on page 4. You might read the question and have the children find the answer.

AFTER READING THE STORY

Ask the group why Jesus might have healed foreigners who were hated by his own people. Help them recognize that Jesus cares about and loves all people and that love of enemies is one of Jesus' teachings.

Encourage your group to imitate the leper who returned to thank Jesus. Have them suggest ways they can express gratitude to Jesus for all the good people and things in their lives.

You might end this session with a litany type prayer. Have each youngster name someone or something for which they are thankful. They can use the lists they made at the beginning of the session. Invite the group to repeat the prayer, "Jesus, we give you thanks," after each statement.

USING BLACKLINE MASTERS

Use Activity Master 4 with this gospel story. Point out the family page for use at home.

The Pardon of the Sinful Woman *Luke 7:36–50*

OBJECTIVES

To help the young children
- learn the story of Jesus pardoning the sinful woman
- understand that Jesus forgives sinners
- appreciate Jesus' mercy and love

SHARING THE STORY

This gospel story focuses on Jesus' great love for sinners and his ability to help them change their lives. In fact, sinners felt drawn to Jesus because they recognized his mercy and love. This is certainly the case with the sinful woman, a most unwelcome guest in Simon the Pharisee's home. Simon smugly points out that she is a known sinner.

While her sinfulness is well known, her name is not. This story has long been confused with the story of Mary Magdalene. It is not believed, however, to be a story about her.

As you share this story with the boys and girls, you can help them see the connection between love and forgiveness. Jesus makes it clear that people who know that they have been forgiven have a greater capacity and desire to show love. Having experienced God's mercy and love, they are drawn to share God's love with others.

The most important aspect that you will want to develop with your group is that Jesus forgives people. Keep in mind that the youngsters are learning about the kind of person Jesus is and how he responds to others. This story provides them with another facet of Jesus' mission — forgiveness. This awareness will prepare them to learn about the sacrament of Reconciliation later in the program.

BEFORE READING THE STORY

Play a word-association game. Read aloud the following list of words and have the boys and girls write down the first word they think of for each one: sinner, forgiveness, mercy, love, Jesus.

Allow time for the young people to share their responses. Ask them what they think all these words have in common. They will probably have no difficulty guessing that these words express the theme of today's gospel story.

READING THE STORY

Use the annotated questions on pages 4–5 to guide the discussion. If you are working with more than one youngster, have them make up questions after reading the story and challenge the others to find the answers.

AFTER READING THE STORY

Explore the different ways people can show forgiveness. The youngsters might respond by mentioning forgiving gestures — a handshake or an arm around the shoulder — or forgiving words.

Point out that Jesus showed us another way of forgiving others. Explain that he let the sinful woman show her love and care for him. He understood that she was expressing her sorrow and love through her gesture of washing his feet with her tears, and he accepted it. This is a powerful sign of forgiveness. We are often angry with people when they have hurt us. We ignore them or refuse to make peace with them, even when they try to make up by doing kind things for us.

As you discuss the story, you can help the youngsters begin to understand that Jesus calls us to forgive others. Through Jesus' gift of forgiveness, they can give and receive love.

USING BLACKLINE MASTERS

Use Activity Master 5 with this gospel story. Point out the family page for home use.

The Return of the Twelve
The Feeding of Five Thousand *Mark 6:30–44*

OBJECTIVES

To help the young people
- learn the story of the multiplication of the loaves and fish
- recognize Jesus' compassion
- want to show care for the physical and spiritual needs of others

SHARING THE STORY

As you share this gospel story with the youngsters, you will have the opportunity to help them become more aware of the extraordinary compassion and care Jesus had for people. They will see that Jesus recognized the spiritual and physical needs of those who came to hear him and that he put these needs before his own.

Jesus and the disciples had planned to go off by themselves for a badly needed rest, but the people anticipated their destination and were waiting for them when they arrived. Jesus recognized the crowd's hunger for the word of God and began to teach the people, in much the same way you are sharing your faith with your group. He told and explained stories.

Another point you will want to emphasize is Jesus' awareness of others. Despite the disciples' requests to send the crowd away, Jesus felt that it was important that they not go away hungry. He blessed the bread and fish and ordered it distributed. The food more than filled the crowd's physical hunger, just as his words had satisfied the people's spiritual hunger.

As you share this story, help the young people appreciate that Jesus cares so much for us that he wants to fill our physical and spiritual needs. Help them to see that like Jesus, they too can show care and compassion for others.

BEFORE READING THE STORY

Talk with the young people about the basic everyday needs each one of us has: food, water, clothing, and shelter. Discuss what happens to people when these basic needs are denied or taken away. Point out the problems of the homeless and the hungry.

Have the group identify other needs that people have such as the need for love, friendship, and respect. Invite them to share a story about a time when they had needs and someone reached out to them. Explain that in this gospel story they will see how Jesus responded to the needs he recognized in others.

READING THE STORY

Invite the children to read the annotated questions on pages 5–6 aloud. Then have them read the story to find the answers.

AFTER READING THE STORY

Discuss with the youngsters how they can care for the physical and spiritual needs of others as Jesus did. What physical needs are they aware of in their homes and neighborhoods? What spiritual or emotional needs are they aware of? Perhaps they will mention the need to be kinder or more patient, the need to be believed, trusted, or complimented. Invite them to identify one practical way they can reach out to others to meet these needs. Impress upon them that Jesus does not ask us to work miracles. Instead, he asks us to multiply his work of care and compassion in the world.

You might end this session by suggesting that the youngsters actually bring food or an item of clothing that they will share with the poor. You will need to prepare a way to distribute them ahead of time.

USING BLACKLINE MASTERS

Use Activity Master 6 and the parent page.

The Passion, Part I   *Matthew 26:1–4, 14–16; Luke 22:14–20*

OBJECTIVES

To help the young people
- learn the story of the Last Supper
- understand that Jesus gave us himself
- grow in a desire to celebrate the Eucharist

SHARING THE STORY

The word *love* sums up the story of Jesus that you will share with the young people in this session. The story begins with the plot to kill Jesus and Judas' decision to betray him. These events provide a framework for the youngsters to contrast Jesus' love so clearly displayed at the Last Supper with the disloyalty of one of his chosen disciples.

In the story of the Last Supper, you will want to reflect on the fact that the bread and the wine become the body and blood of Jesus. The words used in this story are not necessarily the exact words of the institution of the Lord's Supper. Indeed other scripture sources have slightly different words for the institution.

People ritualize their remembrances. To ritualize means to do over, and over again, in a way that gives meaning to the event. Each year we celebrate our independence on the Fourth of July and our understanding of the dignity and rights of all humankind on the birthday of Martin Luther King, Jr. As we celebrate over, and over again, we begin to understand more about what these events mean to us. Because we reflect upon these events as a nation, we become unified as we remember the message that gives meaning to these days.

The same is true of the repetitive celebration of the Lord's Supper. The celebration is always communal. The Lord instituted the Eucharist in a community setting and extended his gift to all people at all times. The celebration unites us to all believers who have heard the story and have accepted the words of Jesus in faith.

BEFORE READING THE STORY

Introduce the gospel by telling the youngsters that they will learn that Jesus asked us to do something special in memory of him.

READING THE STORY

Read the stories of the conspiracy against Jesus and the betrayal. Help the children to understand that there were those who plotted to put Jesus to death. Point out that one of Jesus' own disciples betrayed him. Ask the youngsters to read "The Last Supper" silently. Reflect on the pleasure that Jesus expresses in eating this meal with his friends, and contrast this with the unloving actions of his enemies. Use the annotated questions on pages 6–7 to retell the story.

Help the children to see that Jesus is giving us the gift of himself. Pause to have the children understand that what Jesus said happened as he spoke. Bread and wine became his body and blood.

AFTER READING THE STORY

Explain that we remember the Last Supper each time we celebrate Mass together. Tell the youngsters that the priest says the words of Jesus and that through God's power the bread and wine become the body and blood of Jesus. Explain to them that they may receive the consecrated bread and wine when they are ready.

Each year on Holy Thursday, we celebrate Jesus' institution of the Eucharist. Share with your youngsters how this happens in your parish.

USING BLACKLINE MASTERS

Use Activity 7 with this session. Encourage the children to do it at home as an enjoyable leisure time activity. Point out the family page for use at home.

The Passion, Part II

Matthew 26:36–48, 57, 59–60, 63–66;
27:1–2, 11–15, 22–24, 26, 33–35, 39, 45–46, 54

OBJECTIVES

To help the young people
- learn the story of Jesus' passion and death
- realize that Jesus forgave his enemies
- grow in awareness that Jesus died to save us

SHARING THE STORY

As you share these gospel stories with the young people, they will reflect on the disciples' remembrances of the last hours of Jesus' life. The story begins with Jesus' agony in the garden. The youngsters will probably not be able to identify with the mental suffering that Jesus endures as he contemplates his suffering and death, but they, too, have known fear and helplessness. You can build on these experiences and help them recognize that Jesus turned to his Father in prayer during his agony. Encourage them to place their trust and confidence in God when they are troubled.

We have a different perspective on Jesus' passion than his disciples did as they witnessed Jesus' arrest, crucifixion, and death. We know, as they later did, that God raised Jesus from the dead. The important relationship between Jesus' death and resurrection cannot be over-emphasized with the young people. It is a source of hope to all people who believe in Jesus.

BEFORE READING THE STORY

Ask the young people to recall a time when they felt great fear or sensed that something bad was about to happen. Suggest telling about a member of the family who is very ill, or the fear of getting a bad grade in school. Be very sensitive to the stories they share, which may deal with a family situation you are unaware of, such as a divorce or alcoholism.

Talk with the group about how they overcame their fears: Were they able to talk to anyone? How did this person help them?

Introduce the gospel story by telling the youngsters that they will see how Jesus was helped to overcome his fears about his death. This story also shows us how important God's will was to Jesus.

READING THE STORY

Use the annotated questions on pages 7–9 to reinforce content and encourage participation.

AFTER READING THE STORY

Help the youngsters appreciate Jesus' trust and confidence in his Father. Talk with them about the comfort and strength Jesus found as he prayed. Encourage them to pray often, sharing their fears and problems with God, as well as their praise and thanks.

Discuss with the youngsters the fact that the centurion and the other soldiers were so impressed with Jesus during his crucifixion that they proclaimed, "Surely this was the Son of God."

Have the children pause briefly and make their own inward act of faith.

USING THE BLACKLINE MASTERS

Use Activity Master 8 with this gospel story. Point out the family page.

You may want to duplicate the Stations of the Cross from the "Catholic Treasury" section of the blackline masters for use either in class or at home. If possible, take the youngsters to church to pray the stations.

The Resurrection *Luke 24:1–9*

OBJECTIVES

To help the young people
- learn the story of Jesus' resurrection
- rejoice in Jesus' resurrection
- thank Jesus for the gift of new life

SHARING THE STORY

The resurrection is the central belief of our faith, because all other teachings of the Church flow from the promise and truth of this mystery. As you share this story with the youngsters, who already know that God raised Jesus from the dead, you can help them appreciate the joy and wonder of the resurrection.

In later chapters of *This Is Our Faith Heritage II,* the implications of Jesus' rising will be developed. The message of this session is that through the resurrection, Jesus invites us to share in his new life.

Young people are often quite curious to know exactly how the resurrection occurred. You will not be able to answer these questions, because the mystery of the resurrection has not been revealed to us. Instead you can invite them to rejoice in Jesus' victory over death.

BEFORE READING THE STORY

Give an example of great joy in your life. Then invite the young people to share a story about great personal happiness. When everyone who wishes to has had an opportunity to tell his or her story, explain that in this session they will read about an event that brings great joy to all who believe in Jesus.

Set the scene for the reading about Jesus' resurrection by recounting some facts about Jesus' burial. Explain that he was taken down from the cross after he died and laid in his mother's arms. His tomb was donated by a man named Joseph of Arimathea. Tell them that Jesus' body was not properly prepared for burial according to Jewish customs because it was late in the day and the Sabbath celebration was about to begin.

READING THE STORY

Have the youngsters take the parts of the characters in the story and do a dramatic reading. Then use the questions on page 10 to review the story.

AFTER READING THE STORY

Ask the youngsters to name one way the resurrection of Jesus is good news for all people. Help them appreciate that Jesus died and that God raised Jesus for us.

Point out that we celebrate Jesus' rising during Easter-time each year. Tell the boys and girls that this is the most important time of the Church year. Explain that we also remember Jesus' resurrection each time we gather to celebrate the Mass. You might cite one of the Eucharistic Acclamations to impress upon them some of the resurrection language we used at Mass: "Let us proclaim the mystery of faith: Christ has died, Christ is risen, Christ will come again."

End your session with a prayer. Distribute small slips of paper. Ask the youngsters to write a brief prayer statement that proclaims their belief in the risen Jesus. Suggest a few beginning phrases, such as: Jesus, your resurrection is good news because . . . Lord, I praise your rising . . . Resurrection is awesome because . . . .

Have them form a prayer circle and read their prayers, one at a time. As each prayer is read, invite the group to respond, "Alleluia!"

USING BLACKLINE MASTERS

Use Activity Master 9 with this story. Point out the family page for use at home.

The Commissioning of the Disciples *Matthew 28:16–20*

OBJECTIVES

To help the young people
- learn that Jesus shared his mission with us
- appreciate Jesus' promise to be with us always
- want to share Jesus' message with others

SHARING THE STORY

In this gospel story, the young people will learn that the risen Jesus entrusted the mission of sharing the good news of his life, death, and resurrection to the disciples. He commanded them to preach and teach in his name and to baptize new believers. As you share this story with the youngsters, emphasize that we share the mission that Jesus gave to his disciples. As members of the Church, we are called to spread the good news.

Another important element in this gospel story is Jesus' promise to be with us always. Later in the program, the youngsters will come to know that we experience the real presence of Jesus in the Eucharist, in the other sacraments, and in the Church. For now, you can help them appreciate that Jesus is with each one of us who believes in him, helping us to live and share the good news.

Assure your group that they do not have to know everything about Jesus and the Catholic Church to fulfill the mission Jesus has given them. Learning to be a disciple of Jesus is a life-long process. Help the young people appreciate that we best share Jesus' message with others by trying to live the example he gave us.

BEFORE READING THE STORY

Invite the young people to list the ways they can exercise their responsibilities to live a life of love based on the kind of life Jesus lived. What responsibilities can they take on at home and at school?

Introduce the gospel story by explaining that after his resurrection, Jesus continued to teach his disciples and prepare them for the time when he would return to God the Father. Explain that the story tells us about Jesus' last appearance to the disciples and the important responsibilities with which he charged them.

READING THE STORY

Use the annotated questions on page 10 to guide the discussion and help the youngsters better understand the mission Jesus gave to his disciples.

AFTER READING THE STORY

Explain to the young people that after Jesus gave the disciples their mission, he left them to return to his Father. We call this event the Ascension and celebrate the feast of the Ascension forty days after Easter.

Ask the youngsters to look back over the gospel stories they have read and find their favorite story about Jesus. Why did they like that particular story? What good news did they learn about Jesus from this story?

Discuss how the young people can share the message of Jesus with others. Help them appreciate that they live out their mission by trying to be a sign of Jesus' love and concern in today's world.

USING BLACKLINE MASTERS

Use Activity Master 10 with this gospel story. Point out the family page for use at home.

How to Use the Three-step Lesson Plan

The chapters in this book follow the three-step lesson plan found in the *This Is Our Faith* series.

LEARNING ABOUT OUR LIVES

Each lesson opens with a life experience that explores life's meaning and values more deeply through creative activities and questions. This first step or movement is not just a teaching technique to engage the students' interest. The life experience is a theological moment of opening one's mind and heart to God's word as found in daily life (natural signs).

LEARNING ABOUT OUR FAITH

In the second step or movement, the students learn some significant aspect of Catholic tradition that actually relates to the experience explored in the first step. What is taught may be a story from the Bible (biblical sign), a liturgical symbol or ritual (liturgical sign), or a doctrinal statement or moral teaching (ecclesial sign).

In this step, *This Is Our Faith Heritage II* introduces the youngsters to the basic teachings of the Church as presented in the *National Catechetical Directory*.

LEARNING HOW TO LIVE OUR FAITH

The last step is meant to enable the student to integrate the previous two movements, life and tradition, and to respond in prayer and action. The process is meant to be one of discovery rather than of simply telling the students how the life experience and tradition interrelate. To assist the childern to see how the material of each chapter might be integrated into everyday life, a feature called "Close-up" explores the way a particular saint incorporated these teachings in his or her daily living. These earlier Christians and their stories of faith are part of our heritage.

Prayer is an important part of *This Is Our Faith Heritage II*. Through prayer, the youngsters become open to the Holy Spirit who guides them to incorporate the good news of Jesus and the teachings of the Church into their lives. Each chapter of this book familiarizes the children with a kind of prayer or a prayer form that can be used to deepen their relationship with God. One of the aims of this program is to enable the children to communicate with the God they are discovering. While a variety of prayer forms are presented, they need not all be memorized. Rather acquaint the youngsters with the many forms they can draw upon from our rich prayer heritage to speak or listen to God.

"Understanding Our Faith" employs the use of thinking skills to help the youngsters organize what they have learned. The boys and girls will reflect, analyze, synthesize, and make decisions based on the content of the chapter.

Another way to help the young people integrate what they learned into their lives is through an activity. An optional activity is provided for this purpose.

SPECIAL TEACHING TECHNIQUES

Being An Active Listener

In working with young people, we need to be responsive to what they say and do. Be aware of your students' body language. Fidgeting, arms tightly folded across the chest, and slumping are signs that the they are uninvolved. Establish eye contact with anyone who is drifting. Ask a question that invites the youngster to express an opinion. In this way, you engage his or her attention at a deeper level.

You might also try a technique known as active listening. When you actively listen, you restate what has already been said. This technique helps students expand on their thoughts. An example of active listening follows.

Eddie: I think the apostles were mean to the children.
Catechist: You think they were mean.
Eddie: Yeah, kids have a right to talk to Jesus.
Catechist: You would not want anyone to stop you from talking to Jesus.
Eddie: I'm glad that Jesus stopped them.
Catechist: Jesus did the right thing, then.
Eddie: He sure did. And the apostles learned it.
Catechist: Something important, I bet.

Building Trust

Building trust with the junior-high-age youth is an integral part of creating an atmosphere in which faith can develop. Trust is built at several different levels.

1. Youngsters need to know that you genuinely care for them. Take the time to get to know them on a personal level: ask questions, listen to them, and take an interest in them.

2. Treating the young people with respect builds trust. You also can foster mutual respect between the students in your class by encouraging them to accept and listen to one another, and to treat others as they would like to be treated.

3. Confidentiality builds trust. Young people need to know that when they share something with you, they can trust you to respect their privacy and not violate their confidence.

4. Time builds trust. Be available before and after each class session to talk and visit.

Motivation

The young teens may feel that they are behind, or worse, that there is some shame in not knowing what their peers may know. Your positive attitude and approach are important factors.

Show the young people how delighted you are to be sharing Jesus' good news with them. Impress upon them that you are still learning how to live as a follower of Jesus. Below you will find other suggestions for motivating this age group.

1. Use praise and affirmation frequently.

2. Keep the lesson simple, as suggested in the lesson plan. Success is the best motivator.

3. Have the materials you need on hand. If you are doing a new activity, practice it before class or make a display model.

4. Greet the young people when they arrive. A friendly welcoming signals that you approve of them and are pleased to be with them.

5. Be flexible. Be open to the youngsters' questions and encourage them to share new experiences.

OBJECTIVES To help the young people
- learn that God created people and the world out of goodness and love
- appreciate the gift of grace
- desire to know, love, and serve God, others, and all created things as we love ourselves

---

STEP 1/INTRODUCTION

Learning About Our Lives

GETTING TO KNOW THE REAL YOU

STEP 2/DEVELOPMENT

Learning About Our Faith

GOD'S RELATIONSHIP WITH US

Completing an Interview Outline

Young people are in the process of self-discovery. They are exploring new ideas, forming opinions, and learning who they are. They may be talkative or shy, spontaneous or structured, silly or serious. As you introduce this section of the chapter, keep in mind that the youngsters may feel uncomfortable sharing information about themselves. Encourage participation, but do not insist on it. Your respect for their privacy will help them realize that being Catholic does not involve revealing everything about themselves.

Have the young people read page 12 and complete the interview outline. When they are finished, invite them to share a few of their responses. As an alternative, you can have them do their sharing in groups of two or three.

Talk with the youngsters about the ways relationships develop. Have them write three important factors in forming a relationship. Poll the group once they are done, to identify the five most popular responses. Tell them that today's chapter focuses on the special relationship between God and all people.

Sharing About the Bible

Have the young people take turns reading aloud, "God's Relationship With All People." Use the annotations to guide discussion and clarify content. If available, distribute Bibles and help the youngsters locate the Old and New Testaments. Note different literary styles: the epistles, which are correspondence; the poetry of Psalms; and the genealogy in Matthew 1.

Understanding the Creation Stories

Read through the creation stories. It is most important that the young people recognize that people are the pinnacle of creation and that they share in God's life called grace. When discussing original sin, make certain that the youngsters know that God did not create evil. Emphasize that the power of God's love is greater than evil and will overcome it.

Understanding the Covenant Relationship

Read the story of Abraham and Sarah. If the youngsters seem amazed at Abraham or Sarah's age when Isaac was born, remind them that we learn great truths about our faith from the Bible. We do not believe every detail to be accurate. The truth of this story is that God keeps promises. Urge the youngsters to say, "yes" to God's gifts of grace and faith.

Reviewing What We Have Learned

Review the new words and "This Is Our Faith Heritage."

✦ *Learning How to Live Our Faith*

THE SERVANT OF THE LORD

Learning From the Community

You will find a "Close-up" feature in each chapter of *This Is Our Faith Heritage II.* These profiles of saints give you the opportunity to demonstrate how God worked through ordinary men and women and helped them become models of discipleship, faith, and love.

Have the youngsters read "The Servant of the Lord." Help them appreciate Mary's loving response to God and that she is like a mother to us, leading us to Jesus.

Completing an Activity

As you discuss "Building Our Relationship With God," emphasize that God's presence with us, grace, helps us grow in relationship with God. Have the youngsters complete the activity and share their responses. Encourage them to put their ideas into practice.

Considering the Wonder of Creation

Talk with the youngsters about the many different ways they use, enjoy, and care for creation. Have them read "The Wonder of Creation" and complete the activity. Invite them to share their answers.

Praying Together

Form a prayer circle or have the youngsters gather in a special place you have prepared for prayer. Your prayer area need not be elaborate. It may contain a small table, a candle, and a Bible. Tell the youngsters that Mary's prayer of praise is also called the Magnificat. Divide the young people into two groups and have them pray alternate lines.

Organizing What You Have Learned

Direct attention to "Understanding Our Faith". Note that the young people will need Bibles to complete the first study skill activity. Help them locate the passage from Genesis. The study skill that is emphasized here is the logical thinking skill of recognizing sequence. Be sure to check their responses as a means of immediate positive reinforcement.

The second activity uses a creative thinking skill. The youngsters will synthesize what they have learned and use their own words to paraphrase definitions. As they share their definitions, praise them for grasping the content so quickly.

Additional Activity

Have the youngsters make bumper stickers urging people to care for the world. Distribute markers and strips of white, pressure-sensitive, adhesive-backed paper, cut to 15″ × 3″ lengths. The young people might enjoy working in small groups for this project. This will help build community and also give them an opportunity to share ideas with one another. You can move from group to group as they work, offering suggestions and commenting on their efforts. Allow time for all the youngsters to display their bumper stickers. Remind the youngsters to ask permission before mounting their stickers at home or on the car.

Materials for Activity

- 15″ × 3″ strips of white, pressure-sensitive, adhesive-backed paper
- markers

OBJECTIVES   To help the young people
- learn that Jesus is both human and divine
- discover that Jesus teaches us to live the new commandment
- desire to be a sign of God's peace, love, and justice

STEP 1/INTRODUCTION

 Learning About Our Lives

TOP QUALITY!

STEP 2/DEVELOPMENT

 Learning About Our Faith

JESUS—THE MOST ADMIRED

Rank-Ordering Admirable Qualities

At this time in their lives, young people are sorting out what is personally important to them. The opening activities in this chapter will help them clarify their thoughts and prepare them to learn some of the things we believe about Jesus. Explain the directions to the first activity on page 20 and have the youngsters complete it. When they have finished, invite them to share why they value the qualities they chose.

Recognizing Contributions

Direct attention to the photographs on page 20. Have the youngsters work independently to complete the activity. Encourage them to compare responses with one another. Tell the group that in this session they will learn more about Jesus and some of the things we believe about him.

Sharing About Jesus

Invite volunteers to read the Scripture story on page 21 aloud. Use the annotated questions to involve the youngsters in discussion. Read "The Gospels Tell Us Who Jesus Is." with them. The most important point to understand is that Jesus is the Messiah, the one sent by God to save the people.

As you read "Jesus Is Human and Divine," together, keep in mind that our belief in the Incarnation is based on faith. The youngsters cannot be expected to internalize this doctrine immediately. Encourage them to trust and accept what God has revealed through Jesus.

Learning About the Kingdom of God

Read "Jesus Came to Establish the Kingdom" with the group. Draw attention to Jesus' life as an example of the kind of life we are called to live. Help them appreciate that by developing their relationship with Jesus they will grow in love of him and others. Continue by reading "Jesus Came to Establish God's Kingdom," page 23.

Reviewing What We Have Learned

Have the group work in pairs to learn the new word definitions. Read "This Is Our Faith Heritage" with them and answer any questions.

Learning How to Live Our Faith
SHARING GOD'S LOVE

Learning From the Community

Have the youngsters read the "Close-up" feature on Saint Vincent de Paul and Louise de Marillac. Have them name ways these two saints lived the New Commandment of Jesus. Help them appreciate the great things we are able to accomplish when we respond to the gift of God's life, grace, and live as Jesus taught.

Completing a Chart

Read "Living the New Commandment" on page 26 with the group. Give them ample time to think of unloving situations and complete the chart. As they share their responses, be sensitive to family situations they may not want to discuss with the group.

Researching Scripture

Have the youngsters read "Titles of Jesus". Distribute Bibles and ask them to locate the Scripture references. Since the young people may not yet feel confident about using the Bible, you may want to have them work in groups to complete the activity. Check their answers when they have finished.

Learning About the Lord's Prayer

As you read this section with the youngsters, have them underline the different types of prayer that are found in the Our Father, as each is explained. Pray the Lord's Prayer with them and encourage them to learn it by heart.

Organizing What You Have Learned

Have the youngsters complete the first study skill activity. They will be using critical thinking skills to form judgments.

In the second study skill activity, the youngsters will need to use logical and critical thinking skills. They will synthesize what they have learned and draw conclusions about the important elements of this chapter.

Additional Activity

Have the youngsters work in groups to make a cartoon mural about Jesus. Begin by talking with them about cartoons which have a message. For example, the super-hero cartoon characters work for justice and fight against crime, and the Peanuts characters teach us about some of life's complexities.

Distribute a three-foot length of white shelf paper and markers to each group. Have them spend time thinking about a situation in which Jesus shows people how to live as signs of God's kingdom. What message can Jesus share with people today? How would he do this? Encourage them to be imaginative in depicting the situation they decide on. Tell them that they can use as many panels as they need on the shelf paper.

Youngsters of this age are wonderfully inventive with this type of activity. Encourage them to have fun designing and drawing their cartoon. Invite each group to present their cartoon.

Materials for Activity

- panels of white shelf paper
- markers

OBJECTIVES To help the young people
- know the story of Pentecost
- understand that Christians are baptized followers of Jesus
- appreciate that the Holy Spirit helps and guides us through seven special gifts

---

STEP 1/INTRODUCTION
✳ *Learning About Our Lives*
TEEN ADVISOR

STEP 2/DEVELOPMENT
✝ *Learning About Our Faith*
JESUS PROMISES THE HOLY SPIRIT

Writing Advice

Considering solutions to typical junior high problems and reflecting on helpful people in our lives sets the tone for this chapter and readies the youngsters to understand the Holy Spirit's role in our lives and the Church. Ask the young people to read "Teen Advisor" on page 28 silently and write responses to the letters. Have them compare their responses with one another.

Naming Helpful People

Invite the youngsters to think about someone who gives them good advice. Have them answer the questions on page 28. Give the group an opportunity to share their responses. Explain that in Chapter 3 they will learn who advises and guides the Church and her members.

Sharing About the Holy Spirit

Have volunteers read "Jesus Promises the Holy Spirit" and "Jesus Sends the Promised One" using the annotated questions as a guide. Point out that many people became members of the Christian community through Baptism. Read "The Spirit Helps Us Know Jesus". Emphasize that the Spirit helped Christianity grow in the world.

Learning About the Trinity

After reading "The Father, Son, and Holy Spirit," explain that the Trinity is a mystery of our faith. Use the illustration on page 30. The circle indicates that there is only one God; the three equal parts represent the three persons in God.

Understanding the Work of the Spirit

Read "The Holy Spirit at Work Today" with the group. Emphasize that the Spirit's guidance throughout our lives is promised us at Baptism. Ask the young people to suggest examples of temptation. Encourage them to recognize how the Holy Spirit helps them overcome temptation and grow as loving disciples of Jesus. Then read "The Temptations of Jesus" on page 32. This will help the young people know that even Jesus was tempted.

Reviewing What We Have Learned

Direct attention to "This Is Our Faith Heritage." Have the youngsters review the new words and use them in sentences.

STEP 3/CONCLUSION

✦ *Learning How to Live Our Faith*

GIFTED BY THE SPIRIT

Learning From the Community

Have the young people read the "Close-up" feature on Francis De Sales. Assist them in recognizing the Spirit's influence in Francis' life. Help them appreciate that they can grow closer to God, too, by responding to the work of the Spirit in their lives.

Studying a Chart

Read page 34 and use the chart to help the youngsters learn the seven gifts of the Holy Spirit and how we can live and use the gifts. Emphasize that the gifts of the Holy Spirit are not magical. They are practical, common sense influences which direct us more and more to live as Jesus showed us.

Praying Together

Gather the young people in the prayer area. Ask them to close their eyes and silently think of one way they need the Spirit's guidance or help. Pause briefly to allow them to do this. Then pray the "Prayer for the Help of the Spirit" together.

Understanding What We Have Learned

The study skill emphasized in this activity is a critical thinking skill. In creating questions and supplying answers, the youngsters will need to analyze the chapter and make choices. When they have finished, have them quiz one another, using their original questions.

Additional Activity

Have the youngsters make individual posters about the Blessed Trinity. Distribute poster paper and drawing materials. Tell them that they can create symbols for each of the persons of the Trinity, draw a picture that represents the oneness of the Trinity, or use an idea of their own. As they work on their posters, offer encouragement and praise. If time permits, have them display their posters and explain them to the group. Perhaps you can arrange for the posters to be mounted in a prominent place in your parish for the community to study and enjoy. This will increase the parish's awareness of the youngsters and the young people's feeling of belonging.

Materials for Activity

- poster board
- drawing materials

OBJECTIVES To help the young people
- learn that the Church is called to be a sign of God's kingdom
- want to work to bring God's peace, love, and justice to the world
- respond to Jesus' call to ministry

 STEP 1/INTRODUCTION
Learning About Our Lives
ALL ABOUT YOU

 STEP 2/DEVELOPMENT
Learning About Our Faith
DESCRIBING THE FIRST COMMUNITY

Considering Families

As an introduction to the first Christian communities, the youngsters will examine attitudes and actions which reflect the feelings they have regarding family. Read page 36 with the young people. Elicit from them that the groups pictured on the page are all families. Have them work independently to complete their lists. Tally their responses when they have finished. Discuss with them what they feel is the single most important trait or quality for a family to possess.

Completing a Survey

As you discuss the opinion survey with the young people, be sensitive to those with difficult family situations. Encourage them to explain the reason for their choices. Tell the group that in today's chapter, they will learn how the first Christian communities treated one another like a family.

Sharing About the First Christian Communities

Invite the young people to read "Describing the First Christian Community." Use the annotations to guide learning. Emphasize the specific ways in which the first Christian community was a sign of peace, love, and justice for others.

Describing the Church

Discuss the images of the church. Have the youngsters name which image best describes the Church for them.

Understanding the Church's Ministry

As you read "Christians Carry on Jesus' Mission," assist the young people in understanding that we are called to respond to others as Jesus did. Continue reading the remainder of pages 39 and 40 helping the young teens to see that Jesus' community is called to witness, worship, and service.

Reviewing What We Have Learned

Review the new words and read "This Is Our Faith Heritage." Answer any questions the youngsters may have.

Learning How to Live Our Faith
OUR GREATEST MISSIONARY

Learning From the Community

Have the young people read the "Close-up" feature on Saint Paul. Help them appreciate that Paul took seriously Jesus' call to ministry. He helped us understand how the Body of Christ works together to carry on Jesus' work.

Contributing Talents and Gifts

Read "Building Up the Body of Christ" with the young people and have them complete the activity. As they share their responses, affirm the talents and gifts they name and add others that you have observed in the youngsters.

Identifying the Church's Ministries

Read through the directions to the activity on page 42 and have the young people work independently to complete the chart. Go over their lists with them, having them identify the ministries they are interested in.

Praying Together

Help the youngsters understand that we can ask God for anything we need or want help with in a prayer of petition. Have the young people pray the three petitions. When they have finished, encourage them to use their own words to ask God for help and the things they need.

Organizing What We Have Learned

The study skill for this chapter is a creative thinking activity. The young people will synthesize what they have learned in this chapter and make comparisons. Allow time for the youngsters to share their responses with the group.

If time permits, invite them to formulate their own image of the Church.

Additional Activity

Have the youngsters make wire sculptures of an image of Church they learned about in this chapter, or an original image of their own. Give each young person a 24″ to 30″ piece of bendable, coated wire, available from a hardware store. Also have on hand a number of wire clippers for their use, along with index cards, and pens.

Direct the youngsters to think of the image of Church they want to represent and how they can do this. When they have finished sculpting, have them title their sculpture and briefly explain it on the index card. If possible, arrange to display the group's sculptures in the parish hall or vestibule.

Materials for Activity

- 24″ to 30″ lengths of bendable, coated wire
- wire clippers
- pens
- index cards

OBJECTIVES To help the young people
- learn the marks of the Church
- understand the roles of Church leaders
- want to be a better sign of the one, holy, catholic, and apostolic Church

---

STEP 1/INTRODUCTION

 Learning About Our Lives

AN IDENTITY ACROSTIC

STEP 2/DEVELOPMENT

 Learning About Our Faith

UNMISTAKABLE CHRISTIAN IDENTITY

Making an Identity Acrostic

The young people are increasingly aware that their identity is shaped by many factors. In this chapter they will have the opportunity to explore some of the characteristics that make them who they are. This will ready them to understand the identifying marks of the Church.

Have them read page 44 and complete the activity. Allow ample time for them to work on their acrostics. When they have finished, encourage them to read them to the group. Explain that in today's session, they will learn how the Church is identified.

Sharing About the Church's Identity

Read page 45 with the youngsters. Use the annotated questions to reinforce content. As you read on, emphasize that the first Christians followed Jesus' example in preaching and welcoming all people. Explain that the creeds of the Church summarize the truths that God had revealed.

Learning About the Marks of the Church

Study the chart on page 46 with the youngsters, helping them understand how to live each of the marks.

Understanding Leadership in the Church

Read the story of Jesus choosing Peter to lead the disciples on page 47. Help the boys and girls to recognize Pope John Paul II in the photograph.

As you discuss the section called "Church Leaders" emphasize that Jesus continues to lead us through the pope and bishops. Assist them in understanding the role of the pope and bishops.

Reviewing What We Have Learned

Read "This Is Our Faith Heritage" with the youngsters. Answer any questions they may have. Review the new words with the group. Encourage them to memorize these faith words.

STEP 3/CONCLUSION
Learning How to Live Our Faith
A FISHERMAN TURNED SHEPHERD

Learning From the Community

Have the youngsters read the "Close-up" feature on Saint Peter. Help them appreciate, as Peter did, that all things are possible with the Holy Spirit's help and guidance.

Solving a Word Search Puzzle

Explain the directions to the puzzle on page 50. After the youngsters have located the hidden words, have them tell how each of these words relate to the marks of the Church.

Identifying Church Leaders

Read the text with the young people and assist them in completing the activity. If possible, obtain a photograph from your local Catholic newspaper of your bishop or cardinal. Tell the group that they will learn how men become priests and bishops in Chapter 8. Reinforce that each one of us is called to ministry.

Praying Together

Introduce the Apostles' Creed to the young people. Pray the creed together. Assure them that as they continue to learn about their faith in your sessions together, they will have a fuller understanding of each part of the creed.

Organizing What We Have Learned

The study skills emphasized in the first activity are the critical thinking skills of analyzing data and choosing alternatives. Have the youngsters compare notes with one another when they have finished.

Additional Activity

Have the youngsters work in groups to make collages which show how Christians who live out their faith in the world today can be identified by the marks of the Church. Encourage them to look through magazines and newspapers to find pictures and articles which relate to what they learned about the marks. Tell the young people that they may write original articles and draw pictures of people being signs of the marks to add to their collages.

Materials for Activity

- newspapers and periodicals
- poster board
- scissors
- glue
- crayons or markers

OBJECTIVES To help the young people
- learn what a sacrament is
- recognize that we are welcomed into full membership in the Church through the sacraments of initiation
- want to live as members of the Church community

STEP 1/INTRODUCTION
☀ *Learning About Our Lives*
SIGNS OF CELEBRATIONS

STEP 2/DEVELOPMENT
✝ *Learning About Our Faith*
SEVEN SACRED CELEBRATIONS

Studying and Writing About Photographs

Young people enjoy celebrations of all kinds, but they are becoming increasingly aware of the special significance of certain types of celebrations. This recognition makes it possible for them to make the connection between their human experiences and the seven sacred celebrations of the Catholic Church. Invite the youngsters to read page 52 and answer the questions. Discuss their responses and have them add any special traditions their families may have for celebrating the events shown on the page. Then ask the group to name any other celebrations that have special meaning for them. Explain that in this chapter of *This Is Our Faith Heritage* they will be learning about the special celebrations of the Catholic Church.

Reading About the Sacraments

Have the young people read "Seven Sacred Celebrations." Check comprehension and encourage participation by using the annotated questions.

Sharing About Baptism and Confirmation

Read the sections on Baptism together. Emphasize water as one of the most important signs of Baptism. Use the Rite of Baptism on pages 92–95 with the group if you wish to at this time. In discussing Confirmation, help the youngsters appreciate that it is a sacrament by which we more fully live the Spirit's gifts.

Understanding the Eucharist

As you discuss the Eucharist, remember that our understanding of Jesus' presence does not develop overnight. The youngster's ideas about the Eucharist may be abstract at this point. As they grow in faith and experience Jesus' presence in their lives, they will come to comprehend the deeper meaning.

Learning About the RCIA

Read "Heritage Highlights" together. Explain that this process of initiating new members is based on the way the early Church welcomed new members.

Reviewing What We Have Learned

Have youngsters learn the new word definitions by working in pairs. Present "This Is Our Faith Heritage."

Learning How to Live Our Faith

AN AMERICAN SUCCESS STORY

Learning From the Community

Read the "Close-up" feature on Saint Elizabeth Ann Seton. Emphasize Elizabeth's response to God's call. Tell them that Elizabeth was the first American-born citizen to be canonized a saint.

Completing a Chart

Encourage the youngsters to look back over the chapter to find information that will help them complete the chart on page 58. Check their answers when they have finished.

Writing About Initiation

Have the young people work independently on the two remaining activities on page 58. Help them appreciate that Jesus calls us to continually renew and recommit ourselves to living as his followers.

Praying Together

Tell the youngsters that one of the ways that we express our belief in all that Jesus and the Church teach is through the renewal of baptismal promises. Read each one of the statements aloud to the group. Have them respond by saying, "I do."

Organizing What We Have Learned

This outlining activity will help the youngsters organize and classify the material they have learned in Chapter 6. This is a logical thinking activity. Encourage the young people to skim the chapter to complete the outline.

Additional Activity

Begin work on a sacrament booklet. Each page can be devoted to one of the sacraments. Include a picture of someone receiving the sacrament, a definition, what the sacrament means to the young people, how the sacrament is a sign of Jesus' presence, or ways that we can live out the sacrament in our daily life. Encourage the youngsters to be creative, using original art or pictures from old religion textbooks. This activity can be continued in Chapters 7 and 8.

Materials for Activity

- construction paper
- markers
- old religion textbooks
- pencils
- scissors
- staplers or yarn for binding

As an alternative, arrange for the young people to interview a newly initiated member of the community or the parents of a recently baptized infant. Prepare a list of questions in advance and give them to the person who is to be interviewed. Ask this person to bring photographs or mementos of their initiation or their child's to show the young people.

OBJECTIVES   To help the young people
- learn that we celebrate Jesus' forgiveness and healing in the sacraments of healing
- appreciate God's mercy and love
- want to be a sign to others of God's caring and forgiveness

---

STEP 1/INTRODUCTION

✹ *Learning About Our Lives*

A CARING INVENTORY

STEP 2/DEVELOPMENT

✝ *Learning About Our Faith*

THE HEALING MISSION OF JESUS

Rating Caring Qualities

Youngsters of this age are increasingly aware that they have choices to make in responding to people and situations. In evaluating typical choices they are faced with frequently, you can help them begin to make the connections between their caring attitudes and actions and the healing mission of Jesus' Church.

Have the young people read page 60 and rate themselves with the caring inventory. Have them tally their score when they have finished. Discuss which items on the inventory are most easy for them to respond to. Which are the most difficult? Tell them that in your session today, they will learn how the Church shows care for others.

Sharing About the Sacraments

Review with the youngsters the definition of sacraments. Have them name the three sacraments they learned about in Chapter 6. Read "The Healing Mission of Jesus" with the group. Actively involve them in reading the text by using the annotated questions to stimulate discussion and facilitate learning.

Understanding the Sacrament of Reconciliation

Have volunteers read aloud the sections on the sacrament of Reconciliation. Emphasize the difference between mortal and venial sin. Guide the youngsters to a greater appreciation of God's mercy by stressing that we receive Jesus' forgiveness in Reconciliation. Supplement this section with the Rite of Reconciliation, found on pages 104–105, if you wish.

Learning About the Anointing of the Sick

Help the group understand that Jesus also reaches out to us in the Anointing of the Sick. Emphasize that through this sacrament the Church supports and cares for suffering members of the community.

Reviewing What We Have Learned

Have the youngsters summarize the chapter by learning the "This Is Our Faith Heritage" statements. Answer any questions they may have.

Learning How to Live Our Faith

THE FORGIVING CURÉ

Learning From the Community

Read the "Close-up" feature on Saint John Vianney with the group. Emphasize John Vianney's determination to overcome his weaknesses and help others return to God.

Completing an Activity

Direct attention to page 66. Have the young people write about an experience of peacemaking on the lines provided. Allow time for them to share their experiences with the group. Affirm them for being a sign of God's peace.

Examining Our Consciences

Read this section with the young people. Lead them slowly through the examination of conscience, question by question, pausing to allow time for them to silently reflect and respond.

Praying Together

Introduce the youngsters to the different types of prayers of sorrow. Have them pray the Act of Contrition with you. Encourage them to learn this important traditional prayer of the Church.

Organizing What We Have Learned

In the first activity, the youngsters will use logical thinking skills to analyze each word group to determine a pattern. Then they will eliminate the word(s) in each group which does not fit the pattern.

In the second activity, the young people will apply what they learned about the father in the parable "The Lost Son" to God, our forgiving Father. Have them work independently to complete the activities. Check their answers when they have finished.

Additional Activity

Have the youngsters continue to add to the sacrament booklet that was begun in Chapter 6. As an alternative, you can study the rite of Reconciliation found on pages 104–105. If they are going to receive the rite you will want to make sure they know what to do. If possible, do this activity in your parish reconciliation room. You may also arrange for a parish priest to visit with the youngsters during this session. He can answer any questions they may have about the sacrament, and dispel any fears or doubts they may have about receiving the sacrament of Reconciliation.

OBJECTIVES To help the young people
- learn that the Church celebrates two sacraments of service in Holy Orders and Matrimony
- recognize that the corporal and spiritual works of mercy show us how to serve others
- want to use their talents and gifts to serve others

STEP 1/INTRODUCTION

Learning About Our Lives

LOOKING TO THE FUTURE

STEP 2/DEVELOPMENT

Learning About Our Faith

OUR CHRISTIAN "CAREER"

Considering Careers

The young people you are sharing your faith with have begun to look ahead to careers that interest them. The opening activities will establish a foundation for understanding that Jesus calls us to live out our baptismal calling in whatever career we choose.

Direct the youngsters to read page 68 and complete the activities. Note that they can add careers that are not listed on the line provided. Discuss their career choices and why they chose them. Invite them to share how they believe being a Catholic will make a difference in their chosen career. Tell them that in Chapter 8, they will learn how we are called to live out our faith.

Sharing About the Sacraments of Service

Read "Our Catholic Career" with the group. Pause to use the annotated questions to reinforce content. Have them name ways that Jesus was a sign of God's kingdom by serving others, such as feeding the hungry or curing the sick.

Understanding the Sacraments

As you read about the sacrament of Matrimony, be alert to those youngsters whose parents may be divorced, separated, or in second marriages. Emphasize God's love and care for all people. Point out that one of the most important signs of Matrimony is the exchange of wedding promises.

When talking about Holy Orders, have the youngsters name the local bishop, priests, and deacons and tell how they minister.

Learning the Works of Mercy

Emphasize that all of us are called to minister through service in some way. Explain that the works of mercy are practical ways in which we can serve others. Choose a work of mercy and have the group brainstorm ways they can fulfill it.

Reviewing What We Have Learned

Have the youngsters learn the new words and "This Is Our Faith Heritage."

Learning From the Community

Read the "Close-up" feature on Saint Margaret of Scotland with the youngsters. Have them name ways Margaret and Malcolm lived the spiritual and corporal works of mercy.

Completing an Activity

Explain the directions to the first activity on page 74. Allow ample time for the youngsters to decide who they will write about. Invite them to share their responses with the group.

Identifying Parish Ministries

Read "Doing Works of Mercy" with the young people. Explain a number of service-oriented ministries to them and have them select one to write about. If your parish has a list of ministries, you may want to duplicate this for the youngsters.

Overcoming Problems

Have the young people read "Making Changes" and write a solution. In discussing their responses, assist them in recognizing the vital role the Church plays in bettering society.

Praying Together

After introducing the young people to prayers of adoration, invite them to spontaneously offer an adoration prayer of their own. Then pray Saint John Neumann's "Prayer of Service" together.

Organizing What We Have Learned

The study skill activity, "Getting the Idea," utilizes logical thinking. To complete the map, the youngsters will skim the chapter to identify main and secondary ideas, and supporting details. Have them work in small groups to check and correct their completed chapter maps.

Additional Activity

If the youngsters have been working on sacrament booklets, they can be completed in this session. The booklets can be brought home and shared with parents or you may be able to arrange for them to be displayed in your church vestibule during week-end Masses.

As an alternative, you can have the young people make appreciation cards for ministers of your parish, or congratulatory cards for couples planning to be married.

To make the cards, the youngsters will need half sheets of light-colored construction paper and markers. Have Bibles on hand for them to look through and select appropriate passages.

Instruct the group to fold the paper in half to form a card. Have them look through the book of Psalms to find a quotation that speaks of service for the appreciation cards, or of love for the congratulatory cards. Have them copy this passage on the front of the card. Inside, they can write a personal message. Make arrangements for the cards to be distributed by a staff member who works with parish ministers or engaged couples.

OBJECTIVES To help the young people
- learn that the Ten Commandments guide us in living happy, loving lives
- understand that Jesus calls us to show love for God by loving our neighbor
- want to make good moral decisions

STEP 1/INTRODUCTION

Learning About Our Lives

THE STUDENT HANDBOOK

STEP 2/DEVELOPMENT

Learning About Our Faith

LIVING AS JESUS SHOWED US

Developing a Code of Ethics

Youngsters are beginning to develop a sense of ownership for rules and responsibilities. The activity on this page will help them focus on their own expectations for behavior and prepare them to learn the Church's teachings on morality.

Read "The Student Handbook" with the youngsters and have them complete the activity. You may want to have them work in small groups to do this. When they have finished, invite them to read their lists aloud. Note any common items or similarities between lists. Help them appreciate that living by the rules and responsibilities they named make it possible for them to live together happily. Tell the youngsters that they will learn the Church's teachings about rules and responsibilities in this chapter.

Sharing About Morality

Read "Living As Jesus Showed Us" and "God Renews the Covenant" with the young people. Use the annotated questions to encourage discussion and facilitate learning. Emphasize that the moral teachings of the Church help us to grow in holiness. When reading the commandment chart, take time to explain each commandment and to answer any questions the youngsters may have.

Learning About the Great Commandment

As the youngsters read about the Great Commandment on page 79, invite them to name ways they can show love and care for others. Then, have the boys and girls read "Sins Against Our Neighbors." Help them understand that social sins ignore or deny people's basic rights to share in the goodness of God's kingdom. Emphasize that the moral teachings of the Church help us to live as God's people in peace and happiness.

Reviewing What We Have Learned

Direct attention to "This Is Our Faith Heritage" and the new words for this chapter.

Learning From the Community

Have the youngsters read the "Close-up" feature on Saint Augustine. Help them appreciate that the Holy Spirit helped Augustine to develop virtues that strengthened him to live the Christian life.

Making Moral Decisions

Read "Making Moral Decisions" with the youngsters. Explain each step of the decision-making process. Have the youngsters work independently to complete the activity. If they need help thinking of a moral decision for the activity, you might suggest taking drugs, skipping Mass, or cheating on a test. Remind them that the Holy Spirit is always with them to help them make good moral decisions.

Eliminating Social Sins

Have the young people read "Working for God's Kingdom" and complete the activity. As they share their ideas with the group, encourage them to continue working to put an end to unjust situations in our world.

Praying Together

Review the three basic types of prayer the youngsters have learned: petition, sorrow, and praise. Introduce the fourth traditional way of praying by reading, "We Give You Thanks" together. Form a prayer circle with the group. Invite them to pray aloud.

Organizing What We Have Learned

The first study skill activity involves the use of the critical thinking skills of analysis and inference. When the youngsters have finished, review their answers.

The second activity emphasizes creative thinking skills. In this activity, the young people will apply and elaborate on what they have learned. Invite them to share their responses when they have finished. Emphasize that the moral teachings of the Church help us to live together in peace and love.

Additional Activity

Have the young people work together in small groups to create skits which show how to live a Christian moral life. Tell them they can base their skits on one of the Ten Commandments or the Great Commandment. Allow time for them to prepare and practice their skits. Move from group to group as they work, offering help and encouragement. Have them perform their completed skits for the group.

OBJECTIVES To help the young people
- learn the Beatitudes
- have hope in God's promise of everlasting life
- want to work for the coming of God's Kingdom

STEP 1/INTRODUCTION

 Learning About Our Lives

OVERCOMING FEAR

STEP 2/DEVELOPMENT

 Learning About Our Faith

JESUS BRINGS HOPE

Considering Concerns

As you introduce this chapter to the young people, their reactions to typical concerns of young adolescents form the basis for learning the Church's teachings on hope in God's promises.

Have the youngsters read page 84 and work independently to rate themselves on the compendium for each issue. Discuss their responses. Poll the group to determine which issue most concerns them. Which issue concerns them least?

Completing a Writing Activity

Invite the youngsters to write on the lines provided how they deal with their concerns or fears. When they have finished, encourage them to read their answers to the group. Tell them that in Chapter 10, they will learn how God's promises help us overcome our fears and concerns about life.

Sharing About the Beatitudes

Direct attention to page 85. Read "Jesus Brings Us Hope." Pause to use the annotated questions to promote discussion and encourage involvement in the learning process. Emphasize that in the Beatitudes, Jesus changes our expectations about happiness. Carefully study the chart with the group and help the youngsters understand how to live the Beatitudes.

Learning About the Coming of the Kingdom

Have the youngsters read "The Fulfillment of the Kingdom." Emphasize God's mercy and love. As you discuss "God Helps Us To Live as People of the Kingdom" and "Trusting in God's Promises," be positive and encouraging. Help the young people appreciate that everlasting life with God is a desirable and attainable goal for everyone who tries to live as a faithful follower of Jesus.

Reviewing What We Have Learned

Read "This Is Our Faith Heritage" with the youngsters. Answer any questions they may have. Encourage them to learn this important chapter summary. Review the new words the young people have learned. Have them work in pairs to memorize the faith words and definitions.

Learning How to Live Our Faith
KINGDOM PEOPLE

Learning From the Community

Read the "Close-up" feature on Dorothy Day, Peter Maurin, Mother Teresa, Trevor Farrell, and Dr. Martin Luther King. Have the youngsters name how each one of these people lived the Beatitudes.

Noticing Effects of the Holy Spirit

Have the young people read "The Fruits of the Holy Spirit" and complete the activity. Allow time for them to share their responses. Affirm the faith growth you have seen in them over the past weeks. Emphasize that the fruits will continue to be strengthened in them through their efforts to live the Beatitudes.

Identifying Beatitude People

Have the youngsters work independently to complete the "Kingdom Living" activity. Allow time for them to consider who they think lives in the spirit of the Beatitudes. Invite them to read what they have written.

Writing a Poem

Explain the structure of a cinquain poem. You may want to have the youngsters work in small groups to exchange ideas and pool their creative resources. The completed poems can be copied onto special paper, illustrated, and displayed.

Praying Together

Introduce the youngsters to Saint Francis' prayer by reading through it with them. Several musical versions of the prayer are available on record or cassette (North American Liturgy Resources).

Organizing What We Have Learned

The study skill activity for this chapter is a creative thinking project in which the youngsters will synthesize, elaborate on, and apply what they have learned. Allow time for the young people to read their epistles aloud.

Additional Activity

Have the youngsters make a plaque that expresses their hope in all of God's promises. Distribute a large ball of air-drying clay and a tool with which they can trace letters into the clay, such as a non-serrated knife, a paper clip, or a toothpick. The youngsters will also need a newspaper-protected area to work on, a number of rolling pins, and a Bible. Have the young people look through the Psalms to locate a quotation that speaks to them about hope in God, or God's love and compassion. Have them copy this quotation on a piece of paper. Direct them to form their clay into the desired shape, using their hands and the rolling pins and then trace the letters of their quotation into the clay. Once dry, the plaques can be painted with Tempera.

Materials for Activity

- air-drying clay
- tools to trace letters into the clay
- several rolling pins
- paper
- pens or pencils
- newspapers
- Bibles
- Tempera paint (optional)

Immediate Preparation for the Sacraments

You and the youngsters have come a long way together on the journey of faith. Now some of them may be preparing to celebrate the sacraments for the first time. This section provides a culminating faith experience for those young people and their families. These family sessions celebrate what they have learned in *This Is Our Faith Heritage II* and help them reflect on the next step in the faith journey. During each two-and-a-half-hour session they will explore the signs and symbols of the sacrament(s) they are about to celebrate.

The important role of the family and the parish in fostering and developing faith is emphasized in the sessions. The godparents, the parish sponsors, the principal, priest or deacon, the DRE, and other staff members represent the community that welcomes and supports the new believers. In turn, those being welcomed into the Church renew and inspire the community. With them we can intensify our commitment to live out our baptismal calling.

The larger parish community can be involved in this process through the public celebration of the liturgical rites found in the *Rite of Christian Initiation of Children of Catechetical Age* (RCIA). Publicity can make the community aware of those preparing for initiation and encourage people to offer prayer and support throughout the period of preparation.

DETERMINING READINESS

Are the youngsters ready to celebrate the sacraments? Briefly, let us review the formation process used in *This Is Our Faith Heritage.*

The Life of Jesus from the Gospels

In this section, the young people met Jesus. They were evangelized by God's word, and through activities and discussion reflected on their lives in light of the gospel message.

Enriched Catechesis

Chapters 1–10 presented the doctrines, traditions, and beliefs of the Catholic faith. This period of formal catechesis readied the youngsters to move into the final stage of sacramental preparation. The catechetical concepts for each sacrament that are found in this program are outlined below.

Baptism and Confirmation

- The rites of Baptism and Confirmation show us the signs of the sacraments.
- Through Baptism we are welcomed into the Catholic Christian community.
- At Baptism we receive the gift of God's life and loving presence, grace.
- The Holy Spirit is present in our lives, guiding us to live as children of God.
- We receive new life through water and the Holy Spirit at Baptism.
- We are united with Jesus and share in his dying and rising.
- We are called to a life of service at Baptism, and that call is intensified at Confirmation.
- Through Confirmation the Holy Spirit helps us to be living witnesses of Jesus. The Spirit's gifts help us to become actively involved in building up the kingdom of God.

Defined Words: Baptism, grace, Christian, Catholic, godparents
Correlated Scripture Stories: Jesus Sends the Promised One, The Commissioning of the Disciples

Eucharist

- The study of the eucharistic rite prepares us to celebrate well.
- The Eucharist is the Church's most important act of worship. Eucharist means "thanksgiving."
- Jesus gave us the Eucharist at the Last Supper on the night before he died.
- During Mass we remember Jesus' sacrificial death on the cross. Jesus gave his life to save us from sin.

- The Eucharist celebrates the real presence of Jesus' body and blood under the appearance of bread and wine.
- Jesus is the bread of life. If we eat the bread of life we will live forever.
- Jesus' body and blood nourish and strengthen us to become more like him and to work to build up the Body of Christ.
- Through the Eucharist we are called to love and serve others.

Defined Words: worship, Eucharist, viaticum, service
Correlated Scripture Stories: The Feeding of Five Thousand, The Last Supper

Reconciliation

- The rite of Reconciliation helps us understand the sacrament.
- Jesus brings God's forgiveness to sinners.
- The sacrament of Reconciliation celebrates God's forgiveness and mercy.
- God is always merciful and ready to forgive us.
- The Holy Spirit guides our conscience and helps us to make good moral decisions.
- The laying on of hands and the words of absolution are the signs of the sacrament of Reconciliation.
- We can celebrate Reconciliation individually or communally.

Defined Words: sin, mortal sin, venial sin, social sin, personal sin, conscience, temptation, morality, penance, contrition, chastity, heaven, hell
Correlated Scripture Stories: Pardon of the Sinful Woman, Temptations of Jesus, Parable of the Lost Son, The Good Samaritan
Moral Guidelines: The Ten Commandments, the Great Commandment, the Works of Mercy, the Beatitudes, the New Law of Love
Helps in Living a Moral Life: The gifts and fruits of the Holy Spirit, a process for making moral decisions

As you can see from this abbreviated listing, the youngsters have more than enough background to receive the sacraments. Catechesis is a lifelong process. As they grow in faith, they will more fully understand and appreciate these teachings. Finally, you must look to the young people themselves. Are they eager to receive the sacraments and enter into fuller membership in the Church? Their desire to live as Jesus' followers is the strongest indication of readiness.

ORGANIZING THE FAMILY SESSIONS

Four family sessions are included in this section. The first session is for youngsters preparing for Baptism and Confirmation. The second is for those who have been baptized into another faith and will join the Church through a profession of faith. The third and fourth sessions are for youngsters preparing to celebrate Eucharist or Reconciliation. If youngsters are preparing to celebrate more than one sacrament, helpful adaptations for the family sessions are found on page 46T. This will be particularly true of those young people who are following a program based on the RCIA and who will therefore celebrate all of the sacraments of initiation in the same ceremony.

Scheduling

Plan the family sessions close to the date of the sacramental celebration. Consult families to determine the most convenient time for the session. Consider weekend mornings or afternoons or weekday evenings to accommodate the participants' schedules. Send written invitations one month in advance.

Follow-up

- Arrange for a parish reception following the liturgical celebration.
- Emphasize the importance of ongoing formation, religious education, and involvement in parish life.

BAPTISM — CONFIRMATION FAMILY SESSION

Objectives

To help the participants
- explore the symbols of Baptism
- reflect on the meaning of Baptism
- want to live as baptized followers of Jesus

Materials

- activity sheets for the "People Search"
- pencils
- drawing materials
- paper
- candles
- 12″ × 18″ construction paper
- paschal candle
- background music
- slide presentation focusing on water and the ritual of Baptism
- small, multicolored pins

Introducing the Session (20 minutes)

Greet the participants and briefly explain the purpose of the day. Introduce those who will assist you in leading the session. Play the "People Search" game to help the group members get to know one another. Prepare activity sheets before the session, using the sample below. List fifteen to twenty items to which the participants can respond.

Find someone who...
collects stamps _____
is an only child _____
hates pizza _____
likes yogurt _____

Have the participants circulate, questioning one another and collecting signatures for each item on the list. Give small prizes to those who finish the activity first.

Making Identity Shields (25 minutes)

Have participants gather as family groups. Invite them to make identity shields that tell about their families. Display a large piece of construction paper on which you have drawn a shield. Tell the participants that they can use this shape or one of their own choosing for their shields. Distribute paper and drawing materials. Have the participants divide their shields into four areas. Each quadrant will be used to draw symbols depicting one of the four categories below.

1. a favorite family hobby or activity
2. talents or gifts they possess
3. the people in their family
4. an important person in their lives — a grandparent, elderly aunt or uncle, and so on.

Have family members explain their completed shields. Invite them to affirm one another as they do this, naming ways each person is special. The shields can be displayed along the walls of the room.

Faith Reflection (10 minutes)

Call the large group together to reflect and focus on the following ideas.

- Our identity is a composite of our likes and dislikes, hopes and fears, talents and gifts, and our own unique ways of acting and speaking.
- Each of us is special because we are made in the image and likeness of God.
- Through Baptism, we enter into a personal relationship with God. We become a child of God, no matter what our age.
- Through Baptism, we are identified as Christians, a part of the family of the disciples of Jesus.
- When we are baptized, we receive the gift of God's life and loving presence, called grace.

Family Sharing (20 minutes)

Invite the families to discuss how they have been blessed or graced by God. Distribute paper and pencils. Have each family write a brief prayer thanking God for the blessings they have received. Direct them to save the prayers for use in the closing prayer service.

Break/Refreshments (10 minutes)

Faith Reflection   (10 minutes)

Read aloud the story of the first Christian communities from Acts 2:42–47. Have the group name ways the first Christians cared for one another. Use the following ideas to focus the reflection.

- People outside the Christian community noticed the closeness they exhibited. A second-century writer summed up their impact by writing: "See how these Christians love one another."
- Jesus described the kind of example he wanted his followers to live. Jesus said, "You are the light of the world. Your light must shine before others, that they may see your good deeds and glorify your heavenly Father" (Matthew 5:14,16).
- At Baptism, we receive a lighted candle as a sign that we share Jesus' life. The celebrant says, "Receive the light of Christ." He prays that Christ's light will always live in us.
- The Holy Spirit helps us walk in Jesus' light. Parents, godparents, and the parish community also help us live as children of the light. They light the way for us by their example, which shows us how to follow Jesus.

Candle Ceremony   (25 minutes)

Arrange to have the paschal candle available. Give each family a candle and pins for decorating it. Explain that these candles may be used at the Baptism of their son or daughter. Suggest that they use the colored pins to make a cross and to write their youngster's name on the candle.

When they have finished, light the paschal candle as you pray, "This is the light of Christ, whose life we share through Baptism. May Jesus' light always guide us."

Invite a parent or godparent from each family to light their candle from the paschal candle and return with it to the family group. Ask each family member to hold the lighted candle as he or she makes a commitment to the baptismal candidate. This promise can express how the person will help the young teen walk in Jesus' light. Play background music as the families make their commitments.

Closing Prayer   (30 minutes)

Call the participants to prayer.

Opening Prayer

Leader: "Unite us, God of power and love, as one family. Make us one through our belief in one faith, one Lord, one Baptism, and one Father over all. We praise and thank you, God, for giving us the gift of your life."

Reading of Family Prayers   Invite one person from each family to pray aloud the prayer that his or her family composed. Invite all the participants to respond to each prayer by saying, "You have graced us, O God."

Slide Reflection   As you show the slide reflection, invite participants to reflect on the gift of new life through the waters of Baptism. Slides might include: beautiful water scenes — oceans, waterfalls or woodland streams — that remind us of the order God brought from the primordial chaos by gathering together the waters of earth, thereby forming land (Genesis 1:1–22). Include slides of water sports that renew our lives through recreation; fishing that both calms and excites us as we experience life coming from the sea; the cleansing powers of water that wash away impurities and are symbolic of the cleansing of original sin.

Scripture   Together pray Psalm 36:8–10 (Adapted).

How precious is your kindness, O God!
We find safety in the shadow of your wings.
We feast on your gifts of food; we drink from
    your delightful streams.
For you are the fountain of life, and in your
    light we see light.

Blessing of the Candidates   Invite the young people to come forward with their parents and godparents. Have them lay their hands on the candidates and repeat this prayer after the presider.

Lord, God, may your Holy Spirit bless and guide these young people. Help them to grow in your life through Baptism and Confirmation. Give us the grace to be good examples for them, so that they may always live in your life. May their Baptism and Confirmation renew our faith and commitment to the Body of Christ. We ask this through Christ our Lord.

PROFESSION OF FAITH FAMILY SESSION

Objectives

To help the participants
- learn the meaning of the creed
- explore ways of living the creed
- want to grow in faith in the Church's teachings

Materials Needed

- unlined paper
- drawing materials
- Bibles
- slide presentation
- song
- textbooks
- a large scroll on which the creed has been inscribed
- smaller scrolls of the creed for the youngsters

Introducing the Session (15 minutes)

Greet the families and explain the purpose of the day. Introduce those who will assist you in leading the session. Have the participants count off to form small groups of four to six people. After regrouping, have them introduce themselves and then do a "Question Whip" with them. Call out one statement at a time that each person in the group will complete in turn. Some examples follow. "I'd like to meet . . . . My greatest accomplishment is . . . . If I won the lottery, I'd . . . . If I could be an animal, I'd be . . . . I wish . . . ." Give the groups only a few minutes for every person to respond to every statement. End the activity by having the participants share the most important thing that ever happened to them.

Making Time Lines (25 minutes)

Have the participants return to their family groups. Distribute unlined paper and drawing materials to each family member. Invite the participants to make personal time lines, beginning at birth and highlighting the significant events in their lives. Instruct them to draw a horizontal line across the paper. Encourage them to use drawings and words to note important dates, events, and accomplishments on the time line.

When they have finished, have participants share their time lines with their family.

Proclamation of the Creed (5 minutes)

Ask the participants to name a significant event they are looking forward to. Elicit from them that professing their faith and becoming a member of the Church will be an important step in their lives. Remind them that on this day, they will express their belief in all that God has revealed and taught through Jesus, the Holy Spirit, and the Church. Display the large scroll on which the Nicene Creed has been inscribed, saying: "This is our faith. This is the faith of the Church. We are proud to profess it, in Christ Jesus our Lord." Proclaim what the Church believes about God the Father by reading the first section of the creed from the scroll.

Creation Faith Reflection (10 minutes)

Using the slides you prepared prior to the session, tell the story of the Creation (Genesis 1:1 — 2:4). Slides might be photos of stars, oceans, plants, and especially people in many different situations. Make the presentation as global in nature as possible by including people of many nations, races, and economic classes. Reflect on the story, using the following points.

- Creation is full of God's goodness.
- Because we are made in God's image and likeness, we share a special relationship with God.
- We are called to continue the work of creation by being a sign of God's goodness and caring for all of creation.
- God asks us to celebrate the goodness we see in the world and one another and to be thankful for God's gift of love.

Affirmation Activity (10 minutes)

Invite the families to share how they see God's goodness and love in one another. Emphasize that this is an opportunity for them to affirm and express appreciation to their family.

Conclude the activity by inviting the families to join hands as you pray, "Loving God, we believe you are our creator and that all of life reflects your goodness. Help us gathered here to continue to grow in love and faith so that we are signs of your presence.

Break/Refreshments (10 minutes)

Proclamation of the Creed (5 minutes)

Proclaim the Church's belief in Jesus by reading the second part of the creed from the scroll.

Getting to Know Jesus (50 minutes)

Have each family pair up with another family. Distribute copies of *This Is Our Faith Heritage II* and have the young people locate and tell their favorite story about Jesus. Have the families prepare a dramatic reading, skit, story, song, or mural that retells and explains the story. After allowing ample time for preparation, call the groups back together to share the presentations. Conclude this activity by having the group respond, "We believe in you, Jesus," after each presentation.

Proclamation of the Creed (5 minutes)

Proclaim what the Church believes about the Holy Spirit by reading the third major section of the creed from the scroll.

Faith Reflection (10 minutes)

Ask participants to close their eyes during the reflection and try to create a mental picture of the Holy Spirit. Use the following ideas in leading the reflection.

- We can picture the Holy Spirit as wind or the life-giving breath of God at the creation.
- We can think of the Holy Spirit as fire, like the tongues of fire that seemed to rest above the disciples at Pentecost. The Spirit filled them with strength and courage.
- We can see the Holy Spirit as an outstretched hand, guiding and helping us to live as members of the Body of Christ.

- We believe that the Holy Spirit helps us to grow in faith and holiness. We receive the Spirit at Baptism and the Spirit's gifts are strengthened in us at Confirmation.
- The Holy Spirit helps us to know and do God's will and live together in peace and love.

Invite participants to share their images of the Holy Spirit. End with the song "Peace is Flowing Like a River."

Proclamation of the Creed (5 minutes)

Proclaim what we believe about the Church by reading the last section of the creed aloud. Tell the participants that the Church is called to be a sign of God's kingdom of peace, love, and justice in the world. Have each family discuss how they can work together to be a better sign of God's kingdom.

Closing Prayer (15 minutes)

Call to Prayer Gather the family groups to pray.
Leader: Let us praise the God of life!
All: You call us to faith, O Lord.

Opening song Sing the song "Speak, Lord" from *Young People's Glory and Praise,* (North American Liturgy Resources).

Reading Read John 14:1–7.

Presentation of the Creed Call the candidates forward and say, "You have studied and heard the truths of our faith. Believe in all that God teaches through Jesus, the Holy Spirit, and the Church."

Present each candidate with a duplicated scroll on which the creed has been written.

Prayer for the Candidates Encourage participants to extend their hands over the youngsters while you pray, "Almighty and ever-living God, give these young people the gift of faith. Help them to trust always in your teaching and promises. Welcome them, as we do, with great joy into your Church and help them grow in holiness and your perfect love."

EUCHARIST FAMILY SESSION

Objectives

To help the participants
- understand the signs of Eucharist
- recognize Jesus' presence in the Eucharist
- want to become more like Jesus by sharing in the Eucharist

Materials Needed

- Bible
- posterboard
- drawing materials
- glue
- scissors
- magazines
- paper, pencils
- record for Scripture reflection
- song titles for the first activity, box
- supplies for making bread from scratch or frozen bread dough, thawed; juice
- air-drying clay (optional)

Introducing the Session (15 minutes)

As participants arrive, have them draw a song title from the box prepared prior to the session. In this box are pieces of paper on which you have listed familiar song titles, such as "God Bless America," "Clementine," and "London Bridge." Duplicate titles so that five or six people will receive the same song. If the group is large, you may need to add more titles.

After greeting everyone, explaining the purpose of the day, and introducing those who will help you lead the session, ask the participants to hum their song. Tell them to continue humming until they locate all the other people who have the same song. When they have done this, ask each group to sing their song. Lead the participants in applauding each group.

Faith Reflection (10 minutes)

Have the participants gather in their family groups and ask that an adult from each family introduce the candidate for Eucharist. Use the following ideas in presenting the reflection.

- The eucharistic celebration, the Mass, is our most important act of worship because it is an action by which we unite ourselves with Jesus to offer thanksgiving to God the Father.
- The word Eucharist means "thanksgiving." When we celebrate the Eucharist, we thank God for the many gifts we have received. We thank God for Jesus. We thank Jesus for sacrificing himself on the cross for us. We thank Jesus for always being with us.
- After many weeks of preparation, these young people will soon come to the Lord's table for the first time.
- In the Eucharist we celebrate the real presence of Jesus.
- When we celebrate the Eucharist, Jesus is present in the community that gathers in his name. He is present in the word of God that is read from the Scriptures.
- Most importantly, Jesus is present under the appearance of bread and wine that we share during the Mass. The bread and wine become the body and blood of Christ.

Making Thanksgiving Collages
(25 minutes)

Distribute posterboard, drawing materials, magazines, glue, and scissors. Invite families to make collages that illustrate the things for which they are thankful. Encourage them to use magazine pictures, original drawings, and words in their collages. Have one member from each family explain the completed collage to the group. The collages can then be used to decorate the worship area.

Scripture Faith Reflection (10 minutes)

Tell the story of the Exodus and the first Passover by reading excerpts from Exodus 1:1–15:25, showing a filmstrip, or reading the story from *This Is Our Faith* Grade 6, Chapter 6. Use the following to guide the reflection.

- After Jesus' death and resurrection, his followers remembered the Jewish feast of Passover and recognized that Jesus had passed from death to new life.

- They saw a connection between God saving the Israelites from slavery in Egypt and God's salvation of all people through Jesus' sacrifice on the cross.
- Later, Jesus' followers saw that Jesus was a living symbol of the lamb sacrificed for the Passover meal. They began to call Jesus the Lamb of God, as we do today when we celebrate the Eucharist.
- Jesus gave us the gift of himself in the Eucharist at the Last Supper the night before he died.
- At his Last Supper, Jesus asked his followers to celebrate the Eucharist in memory of him.
- Jesus' body and blood nourish and strengthen us. The Eucharist is our spiritual food which helps us grow to become more like Jesus.

Break/Refreshments (10 minutes)

Baking Bread (25 minutes)

Direct the participants to move to the area where you have laid out bread-baking supplies or thawed loaves. If the participants are making bread from scratch, give clear, step-by-step instructions. Have families use extra dough to decorate their loaves with a symbol of the Eucharist. Attach the symbol by brushing the loaf and the symbol with a beaten egg mixture. Bake the loaves, checking them frequently during the remainder of the session.

Note: If you do not have the facilities for baking bread, purchase small dinner loaves from a local bakery for each family to share following the closing prayer. Use the time allotted here to have the families create a symbol of the Eucharist with air-drying clay.

Scripture Reflection (15 minutes)

Begin the reflection by singing or playing a recording of "I Am the Bread of Life" from *Gather to Remember* (North American Liturgy Resources) or "Only a Shadow" from *Young People's Glory and Praise* (North American Liturgy Resources). Read "The Bread of Life" in *This Is Our Faith Heritage,* Chapter 6. Discuss the Scripture, focusing on the ideas here.

- Jesus is the bread of life.
- Jesus promises us that if we eat the bread of life, we will live forever.
- Jesus shares the new life of his resurrection with us.
- Jesus showed love for us by dying and rising for us.
- Jesus asks us to show our love for him by loving and serving others. All those who eat the bread of life are called to a life of loving service.

Ask the participants to name practical ways they can love and serve others.

Closing Prayer (15 minutes)

Seat the families at tables, which are set with baked loaves and cups of grape juice.

Call to Prayer   Begin the session by praying.
Leader: Loving God, we thank you for Jesus, the bread of life.
All: We praise and thank you, Lord.

Scripture   Read Matthew 26:26–30.

Presentation of Candidates   Call the candidates forward, one at a time, with their parents and sponsors. Invite one parent from each family to present his or her youngster to the leader of prayer, saying, "This is _____ , who has prepared to celebrate the Eucharist through prayer and study." The leader of prayer can speak briefly with the candidate, offering words of support and encouragement.

The Lord's Prayer   Pray the Lord's Prayer.

Blessing of the Candidates   Invite parents and sponsors to place their hands on the candidates' shoulders or heads and repeat the following prayer: "Lord Jesus, bless these young people who want to share in your life through the Eucharist. Fill their hearts with joy as they prepare to receive their first Communion. We ask this through Christ, our Savior."

Conclude the prayer service by inviting participants to share the bread and juice.

RECONCILIATION FAMILY SESSION

Objectives

To help the participants
- explore the signs of Reconciliation
- appreciate God's forgiveness and mercy
- want to be a sign of God's forgiveness

Materials Needed

- mural paper — large sheets of brown wrapping paper or shelf paper
- paper, pencils
- table
- air-drying clay
- drawing materials
- bowl
- Bible
- materials for "In Your Cap" activity
- a church or chapel

Introducing the Session (15 minutes)

Greet the participants and explain the purpose of the day. Play "In Your Cap" with the participants to help them get to know one another. Before the session, duplicate a list of twenty questions for each group of four to six participants. Sample questions are below.

- What was your favorite vacation?
- If you could be anyone, past or present, who would you be?
- What talent do you wish you had?
- What do you treasure most in life?
- What is the most fun you've had this year?

List each question separately and place them in baseball caps or small boxes, one for each group. Have the participants form small groups by counting off. Seat the small groups in circles and invite them to take turns responding to questions drawn from the hats.

Making Family Introductions (20 minutes)

Have the participants return to their family groups. Distribute mural paper and drawing materials. Invite each family to make a mural that introduces the family to the group. Tell them that they may use drawings and words on their mural. Suggest that they include shared interests and something special about each person in the family. Have one member from each family explain the completed mural to everyone.

Scripture Reflection (15 minutes)

Emphasize that we first begin to understand God's love for us through the love we receive from our family and friends. Read the "Parable of the Lost Son," Chapter 7, *This Is Our Faith Heritage II.* Use the story to develop the following ideas.

- God is always merciful. Like the father in the parable, God always loves and forgives us.
- In the story, the young man thought about what he had done and recognized his sin. This is part of the process of the sacrament of Reconciliation. We call this process the examination of conscience.
- When we examine our consciences, we reflect on how we are living. We recognize our need to change and return to living as followers of Jesus. Our desire to change leads us to ask for forgiveness.
- In the parable, the father caught sight of the young man and rushed to hug him. The hug was a sign of reconciliation.
- In the sacrament of Reconciliation, the priest will lay his hands gently on our head, or shoulder, as he says the words of absolution: "I absolve you from your sins in the name of the Father, and of the Son, and of the Holy Spirit."

Ask the group to name verbal and nonverbal ways they have received forgiveness in their families.

Making Reconciliation Symbols
(20 minutes)

Distribute air-drying clay to each family. Invite them to create a symbol of the sacrament of Reconciliation. Their symbols can represent how they feel about God's forgiveness. Allow time for the symbols to be displayed and explained to the group.

Break/Refreshments (10 minutes)

Scripture Reflection (10 minutes)

Read the "Parable of the Good Samaritan" (Luke 10:30–37). Use the story to develop the ideas below.

- Jesus told this story to teach his followers how they could live the Great Commandment. It calls us to love God, our neighbor, and ourselves.
- God gives us the Ten Commandments to help us live happy, loving lives. Jesus teaches us to love one another as he loves us.
- The Holy Spirit helps and guides us to make good moral decisions and avoid sin.
- Jesus' life shows us how to live.
- The works of mercy give us practical ways for showing love for others.

Responding to the Reflection (30 minutes)

Have each family pair up with another family. Invite the families to select one of the moral guidelines, such as the Ten Commandments, the new commandment, the gospels, the Great Commandment, or the works of mercy, and prepare a skit, story, or song that shows how this guideline helps us live as followers of Jesus. After allowing ample time for preparation, call the group back together to share the presentations.

Scripture Reflection (10 minutes)

Read the "Pardon of the Sinful Woman" (Luke 7:36–50). Emphasize the following:

- This story teaches us that Jesus loves sinners and wants to help them return to God.
- In the story, Jesus shows us the connection between love and forgiveness. He tells us that those who have been forgiven have a great desire to share God's love and mercy with others.
- Through the sacrament of Reconciliation, Jesus calls us to forgive others, as God forgives us.

Forgiveness Ritual (15 minutes)

Assemble in the church. Distribute paper and pencils. Ask the participants to write something for which they would like to be forgiven on their paper.

Read Matthew 5:22–24: "But I say to you, whoever is angry with his brother will be liable to judgment. . . . Therefore, if you bring your gift to the altar, and there recall that your brother has anything against you, leave your gift there at the altar, go first and be reconciled with your brother, and then come and offer your gift."

Invite the members of each family to share a sign of forgiveness, such as an accepting arm around a shoulder, a friendly nudge, a warm embrace, or simply saying "I forgive you." Then ask the participants to come forward to a table placed outside the sanctuary, directly in front of the altar. Have them place their slips of paper in a bowl and ask one of them to tear the paper into small shreds. The family may then approach the altar for the closing prayer.

Closing Prayer (10 minutes)

Call to Prayer   Pray Psalm 103:1, 3, 5, 8.
Leader: Bless the Lord!
All: Praise his holy name!
Leader: He pardons all our sins.
All: And fills our lives with good.
Leader: The Lord is merciful and loving.
All: Slow to anger and full of kindness.

Scripture: Read Ezekiel 36:26–27.

Presentation of Candidates   Call the candidates for Reconciliation forward with their parents and sponsors. Have a parent introduce the youngster to the leader of prayer, saying, "This is _____ , who has prepared for the sacrament of God's forgiveness through prayer and study." The leader speaks briefly with each candidate, offering words of support and encouragement.

Blessing of the Candidates   Invite everyone present to extend their hands over the candidates as the leader prays, "Bless these young people who are preparing to receive God's forgiveness in the sacrament of Reconciliation. Help them recognize their weaknesses and turn to God filled with thankfulness for his mercy."

Encourage parents and sponsors to sign their candidate with the Sign of the Cross.

45T

ADAPTING THE SESSIONS FOR INDIVIDUAL NEEDS

The young teens with whom you have been sharing your faith may be preparing to celebrate more than one sacrament. To facilitate the variety of situations you may encounter, three adaptations of the family sessions are found on this page. These adaptations will increase the youngsters' awareness of the interconnectedness of the sacraments and prepare them to celebrate the sacraments at the Easter Vigil.

Session for Baptism, Confirmation, and Eucharist

- Choose any one of the introductory activities.
- Do the reflection that focuses on light and the candle ceremony from the Baptism session.
- Combine the initial faith reflection and the Scripture reflection on the institution of the Eucharist from the Eucharist session.
- Use the bread-baking activity and the reflection on the bread of life from the Eucharist session.
- Adapt the closing prayer from the Eucharist session. Refer to all three sacraments when presenting the candidates. Add the slide presentation and Psalm 36 from the Baptism session.

Use the following call to prayer and blessing.

Call to Prayer   After gathering in an appropriate place, pray the following.
Leader: Loving God, you call us to holiness.
All: May we live always in your love!

Blessing of Candidates   The person presiding prays, "Lord, bless these young people who want to belong to you through water and the Holy Spirit. Help them grow in your life through the Eucharist. Fill their hearts with joy and a desire to do your will."

Family Session for Profession of Faith, Confirmation, and Eucharist

- Choose an introductory activity of your choice.
- Use the slide presentation on creation and the reflection on God from the Profession of Faith session.
- As an alternative to "Getting to Know Jesus" in the Profession of Faith session, have participants look through the *This Is Our Faith Heritage II* texts and select their favorite story about Jesus. Invite them to tell why they like this story.
- Do the reflection on the Holy Spirit from the Profession of Faith session.
- Combine the initial reflection and presentation on the institution of the Eucharist from the Eucharist session.
- Use the bread-baking activity and reflection on the bread of life from the Eucharist session.
- Adapt the closing prayer from the Eucharist session. Use the call to prayer and presentation of the creed ritual from the Profession of Faith session.

Family Session for Reconciliation and Eucharist

- Choose an introductory activity of your choice.
- Do the initial reflection and symbol-making activity from the sacrament of Reconciliation session.
- Read the "Pardon of the Sinful Woman" in the text and the reflection from the Reconciliation session.
- Do the forgiveness ritual with the participants from the sacrament of Reconciliation session.
- Use the bread-baking activity and reflection from the Eucharist session.
- Adapt the closing prayer from the Eucharist session. Use the call to prayer and the reading from Ezekiel from the sacrament of Reconciliation session. Refer to both sacraments in presenting the candidates.

C D E F G H I J—W—04 03 02 01 00 99 98